The Gospel
in Solentiname

The Gospel in Solentiname

Volume I

Ernesto Cardenal

Translated by Donald D. Walsh

ORBIS BOOKS
Maryknoll, New York 10545

Second Paperback Printing, October 1984

The Catholic Foreign Mission Society of America (Maryknoll) re-
cruits and trains people for overseas missionary service. Through
Orbis Books Maryknoll aims to foster the international dialogue
that is essential to mission. The books published, however, reflect
the opinions of their authors and are not meant to represent the
official position of the society.

Originally published as *El evangelio en Solentiname*, vol. 1, pp.
1–136, copyright © 1975 by Ediciones Sígueme, Salamanca, Spain

English translation copyright © 1976 by Orbis Books,
Maryknoll, New York 10545

Orbis paperback edition 1982

Manufactured in the United States of America

Library of Congress Cataloging in Publication Data

Cardenal, Ernesto.
    The Gospel in Solentiname.

    Translation of El Evangelio en Solentiname.
    Dialogues on the Gospels between the author and community
members of Solentiname.
    1. Bible.   N.T. Gospels—Criticism, interpretation, etc.   I.
Title.
BS2555.2.C27713   226'.06   76-2681
ISBN 0-88344-176-4 (v.1)

CONTENTS

INTRODUCTION

In Solentiname, a remote archipelago on Lake Nicaragua with a population of *campesinos,*[1] instead of
a sermon each Sunday on the Gospel reading, we
would have a dialogue. The commentaries of the *campesinos* are usually of greater profundity than that of
many theologians, but of a simplicity like that of the
Gospel itself. This is not surprising: The *Gospel,* or
"Good News" (to the poor), was written for them,
and by people like them.

Some friends urged me not to let these commentaries be lost, but to put them together and publish
them as a book. That's the reason for this book. I first
began collecting them in my mind, insofar as I could.
Later, with more common sense, we used a tape recorder.

Many of these commentaries were made in the
church, at Sunday Mass. Others were made in a
thatched hut opposite the church, used for meetings
and the communal lunch after Mass. Occasionally, we
would have the Mass and the Gospel dialogue in the
open air on other islands, or in a small house that we
could get to by rowing along a beautiful river through
very tropical vegetation.

Each Sunday we first would distribute copies of the
Gospels to those who could read. There were some

who couldn't, especially among the elderly and those who lived on islands far away from the school. One of those who could read best (generally a boy or a girl) would read aloud the entire passage on which we were going to comment. Then we discussed it verse by verse.

We used the Protestant translation entitled *Dios llega al hombre,* which is the best translation of the Gospels that I know. The translation is anonymous, but it was unquestionably made by a poet. It is in the simple language of the Latin American *campesino,* but it preserves a maximum fidelity to the Scriptures.[2]

I'm sorry I can't include the many good dialogues we had before we began to collect them—they were carried off by the wind of the lake—nor some others we had when our tape recorder had broken down. But these dialogues have been lost only for this book, not for those who took part in them and who in some way retain them even though they may not remember them.

The archipelago of Solentiname has thirty-eight islands; some are very small, and only the largest are inhabited. The population is about a thousand, composed of some ninety families. The houses are usually thatched huts, all spread out, some distance apart, on the shores of the different islands. On one point of the largest island we established our little community or lay monastery, Our Lady of Solentiname. To this community came the Colombian poet William Agudelo and his wife, Teresita, and their two small children, Irene and Juan; and also some young people born on these islands: Alejandro, Elvis, and Laureano. Communication with the outside was infrequent, and our contemplative retirement was not disturbed in this place, fortunately hard to reach, outside the paths of merchants and tourists.

Not all those who lived on these islands came to Mass, many because they had no boat, and others because they missed the devotion to the saints, to which they were accustomed. Others stayed away through the influence of anti-Communist propaganda, and perhaps also through fear.

Not all those who did come took an equal part in the commentaries. There were some who spoke more often. Marcelino is a mystic. Olivia is more theological. Rebeca, Marcelino's wife, always stresses love. Laureano refers everything to the Revolution. Elvis always thinks of the perfect society of the future. Felipe, another young man, is very conscious of the proletarian struggle. Old Tomás Peña, his father, doesn't know how to read, but he talks with great wisdom. Alejandro, Olivia's son, is a young leader, and his commentaries are usually directed toward everyone, and especially toward other young people. Pancho is a conservative. Julio Mairena is a great defender of equality. His brother Oscar always talks about unity. The authors of this book are these people and all the others who talk frequently and say important things, and those who talk infrequently but also say something important, and with them William and Teresita and other companions that we have had and who have taken part in the dialogues.

I am wrong. The true author is the Spirit that has inspired these commentaries (the Solentiname *campesinos* know very well that it is the Spirit who makes them speak) and that it was the Spirit who inspired the Gospels. The Holy Spirit, who is the spirit of God instilled in the community, and whom Oscar would call the spirit of community unity, and Alejandro the spirit of service to others, and Elvis the spirit of the society of the future, and Felipe the spirit of proletarian struggle, and Julio the spirit of equality and the community of wealth, and Laureano the spirit of the Revolution, and Rebeca the spirit of Love.

NOTES

1. *Campesino* is literally one who lives in the *campo* (country, field). Most *campesinos* are farm workers, but some are fisherfolk.—D.D.W.

2. The Gospel quotations in this edition are my translations from the Spanish of *Dios llega al hombre.*—D.D.W.

1.

The Prologue to the Gospel of Saint John

(JOHN 1:1–18)

MANUEL read the Prologue aloud. Then we commented on each verse:

In the beginning was the Word,
and the Word was with God,
and the Word was God.

There was a long silence. Afterwards FELIPE spoke: "Christ brought a message from God that was very important for the people, and that meant that he was the Word. But it wasn't just any word. It was a serious word, which didn't deceive. He is the word of God and so he's a true word. And this word came into the world, and has remained among us."

ALEJANDRO: "I think that when they call Christ the Word it's because God expresses himself through him. He expresses himself to denounce oppression, to say: 'Here there is injustice, here there is evil, there are rich and

1

poor, the earth belongs to a few.' And to announce a new life, a new truth, in a word: a social change. With that word God frees us."

I said that was very clear. Throughout the Bible God had been denouncing injustices and announcing a just society, and that had been the word of God. What was new was that the denunciation now came in flesh and blood, in the person of Jesus Christ.

LEONEL asked: "When it says 'in the beginning' does it refer to the beginning of the world or of his life?"

I said the beginning of the world. Saint John begins his Gospel with the words with which Genesis opens—"in the beginning...,"—as if he wanted to tell a new story of the creation.

And LEONEL said: "Then that word is like the promise. Because God had created us with the promise of a Messiah, isn't that so?"

Then spoke my friend ANTIDIO CABAL, who had come from Venezuela: "Here it seems to me that 'Word' has several meanings, and we should look for the first meaning first and afterwards we can find the rest. What is the first meaning of 'Word' here? Probably the text itself tells us. I see that here it says: 'In the beginning was the Word.' That in God there already existed what he now has communicated to us through Christ. And then it says at the end of this prologue: 'Nobody has ever seen God; his only son, who lives in close communion with the Father, is the one who has made him known.' So it seems to me that the

2

first meaning of Christ as Word is that he tells us who God is; because men do not know him because they have not seen him and what is not seen or touched is not known. And so the function of that word is to tell who God is and what God is like. And he has told us that God is justice and that he is on the side of the poor. Christ explained this through his life and his acts, like a single continuous word until his death, and the word, even after his death, goes on being repeated. . . . I have a great fear of talking because I have been very corrupted by the university."

ANTIDIO stopped brusquely. There was a silence, and then I said that, in fact, "word" means "communication." With it we communicate with one another, as we are doing now. And that God also wished to communicate with us and that he has done so in the person of Jesus Christ. That is why he is the Word of God, the communication between God and man.

FÉLIX, a middle-aged *campesino*, spoke: "The word is also teaching, for example, what I teach my son."

And ÓSCAR: "The word of God is also his command: that we must love each other."

And young JULIO: "The word, I say, is a thing that one guy says and another guy hears it. And so the word of God is for us to hear. And also for us to respond to. . . "

MARCELINO, Julio's father: "I've read in the Scriptures that the word of God is like a seed.

Why? A seed you cast it to the wind and it multiplies. And we eat from it. So this word should be multiplied in us. And produce a food. And we should share that food."

We went on to the second verse.

In the beginning, then,
he was with God.

ALEJANDRO commented: "He repeats the same thing again, that the Word was with God. He wants to stress it. He's saying that God was talking from the beginning. Who with? With God. God is a community of persons, and therefore a dialogue. Now God talks with people. This word of God is Jesus Christ. He makes us love each other. It's the word of love."

Through him God made all things;
nothing that exists
was made without him.

LEONEL: "Naturally. Because God and his word are the same thing. Everything he created he created through his word and everything that Christ said on earth was about the work of God. Or better, God created us to communicate with us, and afterwards he sent us his word."

ANTIDIO: "It says that God did everything by means of him. And the Bible also says that God created the world by means of his word: heaven, the earth, the waters, the animals. To create and to speak is the same thing. To create is a way of communicating. In creating you make something known, like when you

4

write a poem or a song, or when these painters of Solentiname, like Óscar or Eduardo, paint a picture, or when a carpenter makes a table. Every worker becomes known through his creation. And when he created light and the stars, the heaven and the earth, God was expressing himself, he was communicating."

I said that the Greek word the Bible uses to say "creation" is *poema*. Because in reality creation and poem are the same thing. The world is God's poem. God said, "Let there be light," and there was light, and so with all the rest, because God created by means of his word. His word became reality. God's poem is reality.

And ANTIDIO went on: "And you always create what you need. Or to say it another way: You create good. And the reality that God created was good. He saw that everything was good. Evil, on the other hand, is the destruction of what is created."

ALEJANDRO: "The worker is the image of God, and everything he produces is good. It enriches man."

I said: "That's the greatness of the worker. The things that we have have been made by God and afterwards by workers. The shoes we wear were made by workers. The clothes, by other workers. The cities and everything in them and the highways and the bridges..."

I was interrupted by a little man with ragged clothes who sat timidly in a corner of the church, away from everyone, and whom I didn't know (he seemed to me to be a foreigner): "All those things come from the power of the Father, and the Father gave that power to the Son, and the power of the Son is also our power."

FELIPE: "It's the greatness of the workers. The workers continue the power of God on earth by working on creation. That's why the workers should be the owners of the earth and not the ones who don't do any work—the ones who have shoes and food and clothing and travel everywhere and don't work or sow or produce anything. But they own the work of the others and the houses and the lands ... "

> *In him was life,*
> *and this life was the light of men.*
> *The light shines in the darkness;*
> *and the darkness cannot put it out.*

FELIPE spoke again: "It's by lies that the exploiters have made themselves masters of everything, by deceiving the workers. That's why the Word of God came to free us from this deceit."

MANUEL: "It says that in him was life and that life is light. We already know that God is love. Love and life are the same thing, because love produces life, and hate produces death. But here on earth love is in the midst of evil. Evil is struggling against love. Lying and deceit are struggling against truth. And Christ brought us love and truth, which is light, so that we too can win over darkness."

THE LITTLE STRANGER: "God said 'let there be

light' through his Son and afterwards he sent us his Son to give us a new light that helps us understand these words."

The true light that lights all men
was coming into the world.
The Word was in the world,
and even though God made the world
by means of him,
those in the world did not accept him.
He came to his own world,
but his own did not accept him.

PANCHO: "They didn't accept him because he looked poor and they felt they were more important. Also because he talked against injustice, which is sin, and they were unjust."

ADÁN: "And they still haven't accepted him. The proof: everything we're seeing, a society full of injustice."

ALEJANDRO: "God made matter by means of his Word, but there are certain people who are enemies of matter, and they're destroying it with injustice. Now I understand better a poem that Ernesto read to us last night, about the stars, that said that all matter is moved by the law of attraction, which is the law of love itself. I say this social system is in conflict with reality. And that's why the exploiters don't want us to see social reality. People who are enemies of reality are the ones who don't accept him."

THE LITTLE MAN: "In the Church itself many still don't accept him. What the light of Christ

7

often finds in the Church is only darkness. Just as during his life there were people who didn't accept him, his word continues now to be unwelcome. That's why there's injustice."

Yet some men accepted him
and believed in him;
to these he gave the right
to become children of God.

THE LITTLE MAN: "Not all of us are children of God. We're children of God only when we accept him. Then we're newly begotten. Born again, we are children of God."

ÓSCAR: "The way I see it, not all people are children of God. It seems that the ones who aren't children of God are the ones who produce lies and are selfish and do injustices. Those are the ones who are set apart."

I recalled that Christ had called those who did not welcome him "children of the devil." And the devil he identifies with the lie: "Father of the lie."

And ELVIS said: "That means that the new birth is when a person is transformed. He changes his mentality. And he begins to do good. That's accepting him."

FELIPE: "I see here that it says that he gave them the right to be children of God. It seems that he gave them the right to do what they want: to transform the world, to create reality as they believe it is just. But there is a struggle between these people and the others, between those who want to change reality and those who don't want to. The same struggle that there was between Jesus and the ones who didn't accept him."

PANCHO: "We're the children of God because we're all brothers. If you draw back from brotherhood you're not a child of God. Anyone who's not your brother is not a child of your father."

THE LITTLE MAN: "People who received his word received the same spirit that begot him, and therefore they are his brothers, children of the same Father."

FÉLIX: "To love your neighbor is to be a child of God. Anyone who doesn't accept the Word of God is the one who rejects that commandment of love, and so he's no child of God."

And the Word was made flesh,
and dwelt among us,
full of love and truth.

I explained that in Greek the expression is very beautiful: "The Word pitched its tent in our midst." And it recalls the time of the exodus when the Jews lived in tents. It means that with Christ God began to live in the midst of our camp. As if we were to say here: "He built his hut in our midst."

THE LITTLE MAN: "Jesus Christ is the word, or the speaker for God, his living word here on earth. That word is for changing the world, and it's a powerful word because with it the

9

world was made. And people who speak with the word of Christ are also powerful. They say anything and it's done."

FELIPE: "You have to keep in mind that they are doing what God cannot do. God gave power to people so he could continue his work here. What people can do on earth God's not going to do. Let's not try to have God do it. What's important is to know that we can do it."

I: "The fact is that as God became man, now man is God. First God became flesh in a person, Jesus Christ, to become flesh afterwards in all the poor and oppressed in history. The Word is now the people. It's the people that do the work of God."

FELIPE: "With no need for God to do it."

I: "God doesn't have anything to do here any more. The work of creation was begun by him but now he's left it in our hands, so that we can continue the work."

ÓSCAR: "Since God doesn't have anything to do here any more, it seems we have a great responsibility to fix the world, so that people who are separated from him and who aren't his children can be persuaded by us and begin to be his children also so we can all be united as brothers. This should be our struggle: to make us all one."

LAUREANO: "It's up to us to fix the world, to establish justice on earth, to make the Revolution."

For the law was given through Moses,
but love and truth
come through Jesus Christ.

JULIO: "Here love is mentioned next to truth. Truth is very important because when there's no truth there's no love."

ROBERTO: "The opposite of truth is deceit. When we don't tell the truth we're cheating. We're exploiting, you could also say."

ALEJANDRO: "Exploitation is the opposite of truth. We're filled with exploitation because we're filled with lies. They've made us believe that evil is good. They've deceived us with propaganda."

GLORIA: "Exploitation exists, but it's not called exploitation. It's called justice."

I: "And robbery is called private property. We've seen then that love and truth are the same thing. And injustice and lies are the same thing. Here it says that the law came through Moses, but that didn't change the world because it was only a law—a religious commandment, we might call it. But with Jesus Christ came a real thing, which is love and truth. And here we're also told what is the nature of that Word that became flesh: the Word is love and truth."

Nobody has ever seen God;
his only Son, who lives in close
*   communion with the Father,*
is the one who has made him known.

11

ELVIS: "He's shown us what God is like because he's shown us that God is love, and to have God on earth is to have unity."

GLORIA: "No one has seen him, but we have heard his Word which is love, and this Word has made us know God."

RAFAEL: "It's all clear."

And I ended by saying: "It's all clear, as Rafael has said. What we've read here is also the word of God, just as Jesus Christ is the Word of God. The passage that we have commented on is one of the most difficult in the Gospels, and now we see it very clearly. This is because it was made clear for us by Christ himself, who is present in our midst. As we have seen here in the words of Saint John, he is the light that lightens all people. He became man in order to make us know God."

2.

The Annunciation

(LUKE 1:26–36)

This commentary was made in the meeting hut. First we had a lunch of rice and beans and turtle cooked by Natalia, the mother of Elvis and Milagros. The Gospel was read by Gloria, one of the youngest girls. And afterwards we commented on the verses.

> *The angel came into the place*
> *where she was and said to her:*
> *"I congratulate you, God-favored one!*
> *The Lord is with you;*
> *God has blessed you*
> *more than all other women."*

I told them that that was the beginning of the Hail Mary and that the angel's first words used to be translated as a greeting (that's what "Hail, Mary" means). But now it's been discovered that the true translation is "I congratulate you." And the prophets often congratulated "the daughter of Zion" (the people of Israel) in this way because she was going to give birth to a Messiah.

Old TOMÁS PEÑA said: "The angel congratulates her because she's going to be the mother of the Messiah and he congratulates all of us because he means that the savior is not going to be born among the rich but right among us, the poor people."

FÉLIX: "The thing is that the liberator had to be born among the oppressed."

JULIO: "It's because he came to liberate the oppressed. That's why he had to be one of them. If he had come to liberate the rich, he would have been born among the rich . . . "

PABLO: "It's not the rich but the poor who need liberation. The exploiters aren't the ones who are going to be liberated . . . "

ÓSCAR: "They'll be liberated from their exploitation."

OLIVIA: "The rich and the poor will be liberated. Us poor people are going to be liberated from the rich. The rich are going to be liberated from themselves, that is, from their wealth. Because they're more slaves than we are."

But when she saw the angel,
she was surprised at his words,
and wondered why
he greeted her that way.
Then the angel said to her,
"Mary, do not fear,
for you have found favor with God.

TOMÁS PEÑA said: "She must have been scared. She was very humble, a poor little girl, and she's frightened when they tell her she's going to be so important."

Young ALEJANDRO: "But there's no reason to be afraid of that. We also could be afraid of being important, because we have to have an important mission too—perhaps being leaders, some of us, . . . to liberate others, to carry out a mission in the community and even outside of Solentiname, in San Miguelito, San Carlos, we don't know."

Now you are going to be pregnant,
and you will bear a son,
and you will name him Jesus.

I told them that "Jesus" was a name that was usually translated as "Savior" or "Salvation," but that now it was better translated as "Liberator" or "Liberation." The Hebrew name is *Jeshua*, which means "Yahweh liberates" or "Yahweh is liberation."

Someone said: "That angel was being subversive just by announcing that. It's as though someone here in Somoza's Nicaragua was announcing a liberator . . ."

And another added: "And Mary joins the ranks of the subversives, too, just by receiving that message. I suppose that by doing that she probably felt herself entering into a kind of underground. The birth of the liberator had to be kept secret. It would be known only by the

15

most trusted friends and a few of the poor people around there, villagers. We have to keep in mind that they were under an oppression. And even the name 'Jesus' was a dangerous name ... "

Another said: "And it's still a dangerous name. And we who are saying that name 'Liberation' or 'Liberator,' we're being subversive too ... "

He will be great,
and will be called
the Son of God the Highest;
and the Lord God will make him King
like his forefather David,
so that he may govern the nation
of Israel forever,
and his reign will never end."

WILLIAM said: "In the Bible, 'God the Highest' had always revealed himself as the liberator of the people. He made himself known first when Moses screwed the Pharaoh. And later, through the prophets, he stood fighting against all oppression. His son, this Jesus, the Yahweh Liberator, will be like him. And he's going to be king."

ÓSCAR: "The angel announces that a new government begins with him. It's the kingdom of the poor. This kingdom has been establishing itself since Christ came to earth, but it still hasn't been fully established."

JULIO: "I would say it's hardly begun."

16

Young LAUREANO: "In the socialist countries the poor person is already king."

Then Mary asked the angel,
"How can this happen,
since I am not living with any man?"

MARCELINO: "It's as if the town of Solentiname asked: 'How can any leader, any liberator, come from us if we're ignorant, if nobody goes to the university and many of us don't even know how to read, if there's only a few of us, and if we don't even have any resources . . . ?' "

The angel answered her,
"The Holy Spirit will come over you,
and the power of God the Highest
will wrap you like a cloud."

I told them that we already know that the Holy Spirit is the same as saying the "spirit of God" (in the sense of "God's way of being" or "God's character") and it's also the same as saying "Love." And I told them that the Church has called this Holy Spirit "Father of the poor."

Young JULIO said: "So it's the spirit of justice, because it's Love. The spirit of social justice, the spirit of change, Revolution. Jesus was born from this spirit."

And NATALIA, who had been the midwife at the births of almost all these young people: "Jesus is the son of Mary and of Love."

And OLIVIA, the mother of Gloria and Alejandro: "Then Mary married Love, or the Spirit of Love."

I said: "Like each of us is destined to marry this same love."

Then Mary said,
"I am the slave of the Lord;
let God do with me as you have told me."
And with this the angel went away.

TOMÁS: "That shows she's very humble. She feels like a poor, humble little thing, instead of feeling proud because of what they told her."

NATALIA: "She was a woman of the people like us."

ALEJANDRO: "It seems to me that here we should admire above all her obedience. And so we should be ready to obey too. This obedience is revolutionary, because it's obedience to love. Obedience to love is very revolutionary, because it commands us to disobey everything else."

3.

An Angel Talks to Joseph

(MATTHEW 1:18–25)

In the meeting hut Teresita read the Gospel
and we went on to comment on the first verses:

The birth of Jesus Christ was this way:
Mary, his mother, was engaged
to marry Joseph,
and before they lived together,
she was found pregnant
through the power of the Holy Spirit.
Joseph, her husband, was a just man,
but he did not want to
denounce her publicly;
he preferred to leave her
without people knowing about it.

PANCHO: "This Joseph was a good man: he
didn't say anything bad about Mary or fight
with her or become violent. He didn't wish her
any harm."

MARCELINO: "I've been thinking about his suffering. He must have loved her. She was his

19

fiancée, she was engaged to marry him. And he sees she's been unfaithful to him. He must have been very jealous. In cases like this there are men who feel they have to be real he-men and get vengeance for the insult. Sometimes they kill the woman. But Joseph, he sees the woman is not for him, and he just suffers in silence."

And while he was thinking about this,
an angel of the Lord appeared
to him in a dream and said to him,
"Joseph, descendant of David,
do not fear to take Mary as your wife,
because the son that she is going to have
is the son of the Holy Spirit."

ALEJANDRO: "He had a great faith in God, because when the angel told him this, he believed it. Another man might not have swallowed it so easily."

TERESITA: "He also had faith in Mary, not just in God. Because he knew that she was a good woman, that she was a saint. That's why it was so easy for him to believe in God who spoke to him through the mouth of the angel."

NATALIA: "And his joy when he knew that Mary's son was going to be the Messiah, that he was going to liberate many people. He accepted him then as his son. With joy."

JOSÉ ESPINOSA: "But also with pain. If the people were going to be liberated, there would have to be suffering too. He knew what was in store for the son and the whole family. He

20

accepted with joy. But maybe he had second thoughts. I see that the angel says to him: 'Do not fear to take Mary.' When he took Mary he was accepting the responsibility of being the foster-father of the Messiah. And that, I say, is no cinch."

ALEJANDRO: "And this is a lesson for many parents of young people around here, who are afraid when their children begin to get involved in liberating the community. Because here the young people are also like messiahs of the community, the ones who get involved and risk suffering for others. And maybe their parents will have to suffer because of them. And the parents shouldn't be afraid."

She will have a son,
and will name him Jesus.
He will be called Jesus
because he is going to save
   his people from their sins.

JOSÉ CHAVARRÍA: "Jesus means 'Liberator' or 'Liberation,' as we've seen. Although the Jews were waiting for a political liberator ... "

"And was Jesus a political liberator or wasn't he?" I asked.

JOSÉ CHAVARRÍA: "He wasn't political. The angel told Joseph clearly: 'He's going to save his people from their *sins.*' "

MARCELINO: "I don't agree. Christ was a political liberator who came to free us from oppression. Because to free from sins means to free

21

people from selfishness, to make people love each other. And if people love each other there's no more oppression. And so Christ came to give us political freedom too."

And JOSÉ ESPINOSA: "If there's liberation it's because there's injustice. If there's injustice it's because there's sin. Sin or injustice is all the same."

I said that it seemed to me that Christ's liberation is also political but different from the liberation that the Jews were expecting. What they were expecting was not true liberation: a Messiah who would seize power and become a king like any other. True political liberation is from sin, or injustice, which is the same thing.

> *All this happened in order to fulfill*
>   *what the Lord had said*
>   *through the prophet:*
> *"A virgin will be pregnant,*
> *and will have a son,*
> *who will be called Emmanuel,*
> *which means, God with us."*

JULIO: "This name that's given to the Messiah means 'God with the poor.' Because if the world is divided into rich people and poor people, he can't be on both sides and if he's on one side he has to be with the poor, with us."

OLIVIA: "Of course. God can't be with the poor and with the rich at the same time, because a person can't be with God and with riches at the same time."

When Joseph awoke from his dream,
he did as the angel of the Lord
   had ordered him,
and took Mary as his wife.
But they did not live as man and wife
   until she bore her son,
and he named him Jesus.

RAFAEL: "The important thing here is to see Joseph's consent to be the father of the Messiah. He agrees to take part in the liberation ... "

ÓSCAR: "For me the important thing is that he was a carpenter, one of the people, one of us poor people. And later they threw it in Jesus' face that he was the son of these people. He couldn't teach people anything because he was the son of poor people."

ALEJANDRO: "Like they would say now in the city to somebody who's the son of a butcher, or of a bricklayer and a fishwife."

JULIO: "Why do you suppose people think that poor people can't teach anything? But Jesus showed that poor people can teach. And also that liberation comes from the poor."

FELIPE: "What I see is that since God created the world people have been divided into rich and poor, and the rich don't believe in the poor and are against the poor."

I said not "since God created the world," because he created people equal, but since we've organized society, because we've organized it badly.

OSCAR: "Then we have to organize society in a more logical way, right? Like the animals, which are all equal. I look at the birds, for example. They're different and they have different abilities, but you don't have some exploiting others. It seems to me that God wants us to be like that. That's why a liberator was needed and that's why this Jesus came, who is God among us."

LAUREANO: "Here it says, 'When Joseph awoke.' Does that mean then he was asleep? Did he dream all that, then, and it wasn't an angel that spoke to him?"

It could be a dream, I said, or a vision, or some other way of understanding things, and for the Bible it's the same as saying that it was an angel that spoke to him. And these angels are still talking to us.

4.

The Song of Mary

(LUKE 1:46–55)

We came to the Song of Mary, the *Magnificat*, traditionally known by that name because it is the first word in the Latin. It is said that this passage of the Gospel terrified the Russian Czars, and Maurras was very right in talking about the "revolutionary germ" of the *Magnificat*.

The pregnant Mary had gone to visit her cousin Elizabeth, who also was pregnant. Elizabeth congratulated her because she would be the mother of the Messiah, and Mary broke out singing that song. It is a song to the poor. The people of Nicaragua have been very fond of reciting it. It is the favorite prayer of the poor, and superstitious *campesinos* often carry it as an amulet. In the time of old Somoza when the *campesinos* were required always to carry with them proof they had voted for him, the people jokingly called that document the *Magnificat*.

Now young ESPERANZA read this poem, and the women began to comment on it.

My soul praises the Lord,
my heart rejoices in God my Savior,
because he has noticed his slave.

"She praises God because the Messiah is going to be born, and that's a great event for the people."

"She calls God 'Savior' because she knows that the Son that he has given her is going to bring liberation."

"She's full of joy. Us women must also be that way, because in our community the Messiah is born too, the liberator."

"She recognizes liberation. . . . We have to do the same thing. Liberation is from sin, that is, from selfishness, from injustice, from misery, from ignorance—from everything that's oppressive. That liberation is in our wombs too, it seems to me . . . "

The last speaker was ANDREA, a young married woman, and now ÓSCAR, her young husband, breaks in: "God is selfish because he wants us to be his slaves. He wants our submission. Just him. I don't see why Mary has to call herself a slave. We should be free! Why just him? That's selfishness."

ALEJANDRO, who is a bachelor: "We have to be slaves of God, not of men."

Another young man: "God is love. To be a slave

26

of love is to be free because God doesn't make slaves. He's the only thing we should be slaves of, love. And then we don't make slaves of others."

ALEJANDRO'S MOTHER says: "To be a slave of God is to serve others. That slavery is liberation."

I said that it's true that this selfish God Óscar spoke about does exist. And it's a God invented by people. People have often invented a god in their own image and likeness—not the true God, but idols, and those religions are alienating, an opium of the people. But the God of the Bible does not teach religion, but rather he urges Moses to take Israel out of Egypt, where the Jews were working as slaves. He led them from colonialism to liberty. And later God ordered that among those people no one could hold another as a slave, because they had been freed by him and they belonged only to him, which means they were free.

And TERESITA, William's wife: "We have to keep in mind that at the time when Mary said she was a slave, slavery existed. It exists today too, but with a different name. Now the slaves are the proletariat or the *campesinos*. When she called herself a slave, Mary brought herself closer to the oppressed, I think. Today she could have called herself a proletarian or a *campesina* of Solentiname."

And WILLIAM: "But she says she's a slave of the Lord (who is the Liberator, who is the one who brought freedom from the Egyptian slavery). It's as if she said she was a slave of the liberation. Or as if she said that she was a proletarian or a revolutionary *campesina*."

Another of the girls: "She says she's poor, and she says that God took into account the 'poverty of his slave,' that is, that God chose her because she was poor. He didn't choose a queen or a lady of high society but a woman from the people. Yes, because God has preferred us poor people. Those are the 'great things' that God has done, as Mary says."

And from now on all generations
  will call me happy,
for Mighty God has done
  great things for me.
His name is holy,
and his love reaches his faithful ones
from generation to generation.

One of the ladies: "She says that people will call her happy. . . . She feels happy because she is the mother of Jesus the Liberator, and because she also is a liberator like her son, because she understood her son and did not oppose his mission. She didn't oppose him, unlike other mothers of young people who are messiahs, liberators of their communities. That was her great merit, I say."

And another: "She says that God is holy, and that means 'just.' The just person who doesn't offend anybody, the one who doesn't commit any injustices. God is like this and we should be like him."

I said that was a perfect biblical definition of the holiness of God. And then I asked what a holy society would be.

"The one we are seeking," LAUREANO answered at once. He is a young man who talks of the Revolution or revolutionaries almost every time he comments on the Bible. After a brief pause he added: "The one that revolutionaries want to build, all the revolutionaries of the world."

He has shown the strength of his arm;
he conquers those with proud hearts.

Old TOMÁS, who can't read but who always talks with great wisdom: "They are the rich, because they think they are above us and they look down on us. Since they have the money. . . . And a poor person comes to their house and they won't even turn around to look at him. They don't have anything more than we do, except money. Only money and pride, that's all they have that we don't."

ÁNGEL says: "I don't believe that's true. There are humble rich people and there are proud poor people. If we weren't proud we wouldn't be divided, and us poor are divided."

LAUREANO: "We're divided because the rich divide us. Or because a poor person often wants to be like a rich one. He yearns to be rich, and then he's an exploiter in his heart, that is, the poor person has the mentality of the exploiter."

OLIVIA: "That's why Mary talks about people

with proud hearts. It's not a matter of having money or not, but of having the mentality of an exploiter or not."

I said that nevertheless it cannot be denied that in general the rich person is a proud man, not the poor one.

And TOMÁS said: "Yes, because the poor person doesn't have anything. What has he got to be proud of? That's why I said that the rich are proud, because they have the money. But that's the only thing they have we don't have, money and the pride that goes with having money."

> He pulls down the mighty from their
> thrones and raises up the humble.
> He fills the hungry with good things
> and he leaves the rich with nothing.

One said: "The mighty is the same as the rich. The mighty are rich and the rich are mighty."

And another: "The same as proud, because the mighty and the rich are proud."

TERESITA: "Mary says that God raised up the humble. That's what he did to Mary."

And MARIÍTA: "And what he did to Jesus who was poor and to Mary, and to all the others who followed Jesus, who were poor."

I asked what they thought Herod would have said if he had known that a woman of the people had sung that God had pulled down the mighty and raised up the humble, filled the hungry with good things and left the rich with nothing.

NATALIA laughed and said: "He'd say she was crazy."

ROSITA: "That she was a communist."

LAUREANO: "The point isn't that they would just *say* the Virgin was a communist. She *was* a communist."

"And what would they say in Nicaragua if they heard what we're saying here in Solentiname?"

Several voices: "That we're communists."

Someone asked: "That part about filling the hungry with good things?"

A young man answered: "The hungry are going to eat."

And another: "The Revolution."

LAUREANO: "That is the Revolution. The rich person or the mighty is brought down and the poor person, the one who was down, is raised up."

Still another: "If God is against the mighty, then he has to be on the side of the poor."

ANDREA, Óscar's wife, asked: "That promise that the poor would have those good things, was it for then, for Mary's time, or would it happen in our time? I ask because I don't know."

One of the young people answered: "She spoke for the future, it seems to me, because we are just barely beginning to see the liberation she announces."

He helps the nation of Israel his servant,
in remembrance of his love;
as he had promised to our fathers,
to Abraham, and to his descendants
*   forever.*

ALEJANDRO: "That nation of Israel that she speaks about is the new people that Jesus formed, and we are this people."

WILLIAM: "It's the people who will be liberated, like before the other people were liberated from the dictatorship of Egypt, where they were treated like shit, changed into cheap hand labor. But the people can't be liberated by others. They must liberate themselves. God can show the way to the Promised Land, but the people themselves must begin the journey."

ÓSCAR asked: "Can you take riches from the rich by force? Christ didn't force the rich young man. He said to him: 'If you wish . . . ' "

I thought for a while before answering. I said hesitantly: "You might let him go to another country . . ."

WILLIAM: "But not let him take his wealth with him."

FELIPE: "Yes, let him take it."

The last remark was from MARÍITA: "Mary sang here about equality. A society with no social classes. Everyone alike."

5.

The Song of Zacharias

(LUKE 1:67–80)

In the hut again. We were going to comment on the song that Zacharias wrote at the birth of his son, John the Baptist.

Blessed be the Lord God of Israel;
for he has come to us who are his people
and has saved us.

MARÍITA: "They were a people without hope. He's given them good news, about a liberation. The oppression they were under was caused by selfishness. And God came to save them from selfishness."

FELIPE: "He came to save us with the new teaching of John. John was filled with the Holy Spirit, which is love. And his teaching was equality, to put an end to the differences between people—the idea that some are masters and others are slaves, or peasants, which is the same."

I: "God had already brought the people out of

the oppression of Egypt, and he brought them to a land where they were going to be free. He ordered them to have no poor among them. But there they began to have injustices and to oppress one another. That's why there was need for a new liberation."

He has given us a powerful savior
from among the descendants
of his servant David.

ALEJANDRO: "David was a king. This means that the Messiah was going to be a king too."

DON JOSÉ: "That king business, it seems to me that his teaching is going to rule. I mean that love among people will rule. There won't be any exploitation or anything like it."

GLORIA: "What's going to rule is the Revolution."

MANUEL: "That's what Christ meant when he said that his kingdom was not of this world. The radio is talking about the scandal of the white slave traffic in our capital, Managua. There they hold the women as prisoners in the bars. They even guard them with police. They won't even let them go out to the corner. One of them told the reporters that she'd been sold for four hundred *pesos*. And this is just like the people who are ignorant, illiterate, poorly fed. And doctors for us country people? There isn't a single doctor! No, the kingdom of Christ is completely different from this system. That's why he said it was another world."

So he promised it through his holy prophets
  from ancient times:
that he was going to save us
  from our enemies,
and from all who hate us.

Little ADÁN: "The enemies it talks about are the enemies of the poor. Those are the ones that hate us."

DONALD: "People thought that the Messiah was going to come to liberate the people from those exploiters, that Mafia . . . "

FELIPE: "It seems to me that thinking is different today. God isn't going to liberate us. We have to do it ourselves, with our own efforts. Let's get on with it! And let's not wait for God to liberate us without us taking part in the liberation."

ÓSCAR: "God isn't going to liberate us?"

FELIPE: "Yes, but working through us with the teaching he has given us."

And I said that in reality God doesn't liberate us directly but through the Messiah. And now the Messiah isn't only Jesus but all of us, and that's why he's also called Emmanuel, which means "God with us." Liberation is accomplished by God working through us, as Felipe said.

And that he would take pity
  on our ancestors,
and that he would not forget
  his holy covenant.

WILLIAM: "This seems very interesting to me—that liberation is also for the dead. Because those women Manuel told us about, the ones held captive in bars, if they die there, isn't there any hope of Revolution for them? Liberation can't be only for people who are alive when it happens. That wouldn't be fair."

ROBERT PRING-MILL, Lecturer in Literature at Oxford, who was visiting us, said: "That would be elitist, wouldn't it? Here it's talking about a covenant, the one that God made with his people. If they obeyed his law he would bring them to a land of liberty, the Promised Land. Now Christ brought a new covenant and anyone who obeys his law, which is the law of love, will live even though he is dead."

So that we may serve him without fear,
just and dedicated to him
all the days of our life.

ALEJANDRO: "We have to serve God through love and not through fear. We should be dedicated to him but without fear. And we shouldn't be afraid of people either, and because we're afraid not serve God and be dedicated to him."

FELIPE: "We've heard it said that he liberates us from our enemies and from everyone that hates us. I think this also means to liberate us from the teachings of our enemies, from the ideas that keep us alienated, so that we can accept the teachings of Christ. Our enemies are the ones who are exploiting us, right? And

36

we must liberate ourselves from their teachings and from our fear of them."

DONALD: "I find that to serve God without fear is to love our neighbor and to serve him, without fear of the others, of the authorities, for example ... "

WILLIAM: "I believe that the two things work together, loving and not being afraid. The more you love the more you get rid of fear. Yesterday we were reading with the boys in the Youth Club the diary of that young guerrilla fighter Néstor Paz, a mystic in love with God, who died in the Bolivian guerrilla war. And there he spoke about the possibility of being shot at any moment. He knew that they had lost the war, and still he was very calm. He saw God in every other person, and he understood love as an urgency to solve the other fellow's problem. Because of that total surrender, because of that love, he had no fear of death and they couldn't do him any harm ... "

ROBERT PRING-MILL: "It says 'just and dedicated to him.' The word 'just' refers to a way of dealing with one's neighbor. 'Dedicated to God' comes to the same thing. It may be difficult to understand what 'just' means. We can understand it better through its opposite, 'injustice.' When we see an injustice we recognize it immediately. The just person is the one who is free of that. And by the same token he also struggles against it. He wants to free others from injustice. Here we have been saying that we must have a just and fearless life, which is equivalent to a loving and fearless life."

I said that when humanity is totally just all those who have led just lives and have contributed to justice will be living in justice even though they have died, as Roberto reminded us. How that will be we do not know. It will be, it seems to me, like the presence of Christ, who, although he died, is in our midst.

> *And you, my son, will be called the prophet*
>   *of God the Highest:*
> *for you will go before the Lord*
>   *to prepare his ways,*
> *to let the people know that their sins*
>   *will be forgiven*
> *and that so they will receive salvation.*

OLIVIA: "What John was preaching was a change of attitude. To put an end to injustice, that's a change of attitude. And this is to prepare the way—the way along which liberation will come. It's up to us to prepare the way too, I mean, to make society change. Not only society off there in Managua but also right here in Solentiname, because us poor people are also alienated. And it's up to us, like to John, to announce the coming of the Liberator."

> *For our God in his love and mercy*
> *gives us from on high the sun of a new day,*
> *to bring light to those who live in darkness*
> *and in the shadow of death.*

JULIO: "The darkness is selfishness. People

who exploit others are the ones who live in darkness. And they don't live happily. The rich don't live happily. They live in death."

ÁNGEL: "It seems to me it's not just the rich. The poor, too. Those of us who don't struggle, who don't cooperate, we're in darkness too, I think."

NATALIA: "The one who's shut up in himself even though he's not rich."

ÓSCAR: "It happens to all of us. Although it doesn't happen the same way to the exploiters as to the poor. If a poor man is unjust to another, he's acting like a rich man toward him. But the rich man always acts like a rich man."

And to guide our steps
along the way of peace.

JULIO: "It seems to me that peace can exist only when not just Nicaragua but all the other countries are free. It seems to me that it's not a question of waiting for a Christ, as many of us perhaps are waiting. It seems to me that when we have love for each other, there will be peace. Because right now we don't have much love."

MANUEL: "Love and justice, which we have seen are the same thing, will bring peace. Hatred and injustice produce war. When men live like brothers there will be peace. When in a household everyone loves everyone else, they are at peace. There are no quarrels."

I told them that the previous night Radio Havana had announced that the Vietnam War had ended. Even though there cannot be a true peace while capitalism and imperialism exist, Christ has come to guide us along the path of peace, as this song of Zacharias has said, that is, if we follow his teachings.

MARIÍTA adds: "But we haven't followed them, and that's why there's been no peace."

And LAUREANO: "But when they are followed, in socialist society, there will be peace."

6.

The Birth of Jesus

(LUKE 2:6–7)

And it happened
that while they were in Bethlehem
the time came for Mary to give birth.
She bore her first-born son,
and wrapped him in swaddling clothes,
and laid him in the manger because
*   there was no room for them in the inn.*

At midnight we were in the little church in
Solentiname celebrating Christmas Mass. The
day before Managua had been destroyed by
the earthquake. I told them that the wealth of
the country was concentrated there alongside
the greatest misery in the country. Certainly
the Christmas that they were preparing to
celebrate there was not the Christ Mass but
the Money-God Mass. The tragedy in Managua tonight, and in the whole country, is very
much like the painful scene described in the
Gospel: Mary homeless and having to give
birth to the Son of God surrounded by animals.

I also told them that a few hours before the earthquake a group of boys and girls had gathered in the atrium of the cathedral to begin a three-day fast in protest against social injustices: malnutrition, lack of housing, exploitation of laborers, thefts from the people. . . . And they were asking for a Christmas without political prisoners.

REBECA spoke: "From the moment of his birth, God chose conditions like the poorest person, didn't he? I don't think God wants great banquets or a lot of money, as Ernesto has said, or for business to make profits off the celebration of his birth. He wants us to wait for him maybe like Nicaragua is waiting right now, because he was born as a poor child and he wants us all to be poor, right? Or for us to be all equal, and he doesn't want us to do what they used to do in Managua, where Christmas was only a celebration to spend money (for the ones who had money), to have a good time, to dance or anything. They weren't celebrating his coming. That's what I believe . . . "

And another one added: "The Scriptures are perfectly clear, man. The fact is that Christ was born as a poor little child, like the humblest person. The Scriptures keep telling us this and I don't understand why we don't see it."

Another said: "These facts hurt our consciences and bring us closer to him. Because us humans easily get off the track and we need very strong shocks to be able to change."

PEDRO RAFAEL GUTIÉRREZ, a Managua journalist who has been studying with us for two months, said: "I'm practically a stranger among you (it's exactly two months since I arrived in Cosme Canales' boat), but I already feel a great affection for you all, for Octavio, Tomás Peña, Doña Justa, Laureano, Alejandro, William, Tere, Ernesto, and I'm sorry to have to leave you now to go back to the ruins of Managua to search for my family. You are really poor people, but there I'll find people poorer than you, without water, without electricity, without food, even without a communion like this one. I hope that this tremendous grief in Managua will be a rebirth. Innocents died in Managua like innocents died when Christ was born. But Christ lived, which is what matters. I hope that we can profit there from this terrible Christmas to bring about a *total* change. And I want to say goodbye."

JOSÉ the carpenter spoke: "The change has to be for everybody. We shouldn't try to dominate each other either. Just now we read that Jesus was born poor, among the animals. He was born there for a reason ... "

Old TOMÁS PEÑA, who besides being a farmer is a good fisherman: "To teach us not to seek riches, not to have a big house to have a child in, right? Just what's natural."

I said that Pedro was right in speaking of this painful Managua Christmas as a rebirth. At the Last Supper Christ also spoke of his death as a birth. Every woman suffers great pain

43

when she is going to give birth, he said, but afterwards she is filled with joy when the child is born. This is how he explained his death and also all human tragedy. Women understand these things better. And his mother Mary would understand it very well, Mary who had her labor pains in a stable on the first Christmas. Perhaps he said this especially for her since she would suffer so much during his passion. But he said it for all of us too. Human tragedy has meaning. It is for a birth.

JULIO: "But maybe the suffering in Managua will just help the Christians, just the ones who understand. And not those who don't understand."

Another young man: "Tragedy is for everybody, understand it or not, and the birth is for everybody. Even though Christians are the only ones maybe who can understand tragedy."

FELIPE, the son of Tomás Peña, turned to me and said: "I believe, Ernesto, that Jesus Christ has done this on this Christmas because more than anything else he likes equality. In Managua a lot of people were planning a very merry Christmas, even though others were suffering, and if the tragedy had not happened in Managua, if it had been out in the country, they wouldn't be sad. But since it's Managua that has been destroyed, now we're all living through the same thing, we're all feeling the grief that everybody else is."

And PEDRO RAFAEL GUTIÉRREZ, the journalist: "What Felipe has said is very beautiful. Christmas last year was a very merry Christmas in Managua. The rich had huge turkeys, very pretty Christmas trees, and a lot of decorations and lights in their houses. But neighborhoods like Acahualinca didn't have a thing. There was more misery there than out in the country. This year again there's nothing in Acahualinca, but the rich don't have anything either. Tragedy made us equal. For the first time in the history of Nicaragua rich and poor shared the tragedy, which used to be shared only by the poor. And this is the most wonderful thing that has happened, because tragedy has brought us all together as equals."

ALEJANDRO: "We should clear one thing up. Let's not be happy because there was tragedy for everybody. The best thing would be for nobody to suffer. Let everybody have enough to be happy at Christmastime. Just to clear it up a bit."

I said that the goal is to conquer tragedy, even death. We Christians believe that one day death will be defeated (by life, which is to say, by love). From now on with love we can triumph over illness, ignorance, misery, and even the catastrophes of nature. At the moment we have a social system that cannot solve these problems. The city had a terrible misfortune, with a selfish, individualistic system like capitalism in which each one goes off on his own pursuing his own interests. And there isn't any unity or cooperation like you find among certain animals like ants and bees. In a society of solidarity and not of selfishness like this one, people can defend themselves perfectly well against natural catastrophes like the eruption of a volcano or an earthquake. Jesus came to earth precisely for this reason. He was born into a humanity divided and dominated by crime in order to unite us and to change the order of things. And that's where we are . . .

FÉLIX interrupted me: "I believe that what happened in Managua had to happen because of the sins . . . "

OLIVIA: "The earthquake didn't happen because of sins. But the consequences of the earthquake did happen because of sins, because sins are selfishness."

JULIO: "Sufferings aren't God's punishment, because the poor are always the ones who suffer most. If you're rich you pay for a car, a plane, and you get out of the city. You don't have any problem."

"I think it doesn't even do the President any good to be rich right now," said another, "because he's a man who has very wrong ideas about his money. And when a part of the presidential palace fell down he thought he was dying and he wasn't."

PEDRO RAFAEL GUTIÉRREZ spoke again: "I think that in this earthquake the ones who are suffering most are the rich, and I'm going to tell you why: Acahualinca has never had any water, any electricity, any milk, any rice, any beans. Now this Christmas the rest of them don't have any either. But the poor have been without food and electricity for a long time. All their Christmases have been like this. The radio talks about people going out into the street without shoes or clothes, and how the hell long have the poor people gone without shoes and clothes?"

"They've been like that since the birth of Jesus ... "

FÉLIX spoke again: "I'm going to tell you one thing. Listen to me, Pedro. The rich never suffer. The government puts a five per cent tax on business. And are they the ones who pay it? It's the poor. And tell me, who are the workers in Nicaragua if the poor aren't? Who creates all the business in Nicaragua? Isn't it the people that pay for it? And then this crisis comes. And who do they gouge for it? The ones that pay are us, the *campesinos*, the poor who work in Nicaragua."

Outside there was a lovely full moon and on both sides of the little church the lake was calm. Now it was just the young people who went on talking.

"We're not the only poor ones. Managua was full of poor people, not just the rich. Most of the laborers in the country were there. And there are poor people everywhere."

"He came to share the lot of the poor. And

47

Joseph and Mary were turned away from the inn because they were poor. If they'd been rich they'd have been welcomed in."

"God wanted his son to be born in a pigsty, in a stable. . . . He wanted his son to belong to the poor class, right? If God had wanted him to be born to a rich lady, that lady would have had a room reserved at that hotel. Especially arriving in her condition."

"I see in this the humility of God. Because it was his son, and his mother had him just like any dog. And Jesus came to free the world from these injustices (which still exist). And he came so that we could be united and struggle against these injustices. . . . Because we go right on being like that, with somebody's foot on our neck. And the rich, how do they look at us? They look down on us. That's why we've got to get together to win. Or even all be a single revolutionary. Like Christ. He was the greatest revolutionary, because being God he identified with the poor and he came down from heaven to become a member of the lower class and he gave his life for us all. The way I see it, we all ought to struggle like that for other people and be like him. Get together and be brave. That way nobody will be without a house, and even if an earthquake knocks his house down he'll get another one. And nobody will have to go on being humiliated by the rich."

"With today's Gospel, it seems to me that no poor person should feel looked down upon. It seems to me that it's clear that a poor person is more important than a rich one. Christ is with us poor people. I think we're worth more. To God. To the rich we aren't worth a thing, good only to work for them."

"Well, God is showing us with this Gospel that the rich think of us as dirt. Like we have no value. For them we don't exist. Here we see that's the way they treated his son, with no consideration. Not even a roof over his head or a cot to sleep on."

"The poor person supports the rich ones because if he didn't work they wouldn't be anything. But the rich take advantage of the poor, and when they have their banquets they go off by themselves. They don't know that everything they have comes through the poor. They think they get things done through their money, but it's through the poor person's work. And of course when they have their banquets they forget all about you. They think banquets are only for them. They don't know that without us they wouldn't be worth anything."

"Jesus was rejected in Bethlehem because he was poor, and he goes on being rejected in the world for that same reason. Because when you come down to it the poor person is always rejected. In our system, that is."

"But now this Christmas Managua doesn't have any houses, just like Jesus in Bethlehem was born without a house. And there are no Christmas banquets just like there wasn't any banquet in Bethlehem when Jesus was born.

Now this Christmas seems to me more Christian, and it can help raise our consciousness. And maybe someday everybody will have a house and everybody will be happy and nobody will be rejected."

At the end they talked about taking up a collection for Managua. Some offered corn, others rice, beans. Félix asked me if I was going to Managua the next day. I told him I would try to go (I had no news of my family either), although I didn't know if there was any transportation to get there.

"When there's no transportation we walk."

7.

The Shepherds of Bethlehem

(LUKE 2:8–20)

Near Bethlehem there were some shepherds
who were spending the night in the field,
watching over their sheep.
Suddenly an angel of the Lord appeared,
and the glory of the Lord shone round
*   them: and they were very frightened.*
But the angel said to them,
"Don't be afraid, for I bring you good news
that will be cause for much joy for all."

We were gathered in the little church. The
first to speak was old TOMÁS PEÑA, with his
customary wonderful simplicity: "The way I
see it is that those guys who were watching
over their sheep heard good news. There they
were just like us here, and they heard good
news. Like when we heard that you were coming. They told us that a priest was coming and
we couldn't believe it at first, because no priest
ever used to come here. . . . Well, it was like
this when they were watching over their

51

sheep and they heard good news. They were sad before. They weren't at a party. They were just screwed up."

"And why were they the ones to get the good news?" I asked.

TOMÁS PEÑA: "Because they were closer to God. Others were thinking about bad things, and not good things. That's how it seems to me."

PATRICIO: "They were closer to God because they were there at night keeping watch, and since they were keeping watch God wanted to send them good news. It seems to me that that's the way it might have been."

FELIPE: "The angel came to them because they were working men, and I find this is very important for us. Because they were poor little people who were working. They were watching over their sheep which is like taking care of cattle today. They were workers, laborers, poor people. The angel of God could have gone to the king's palace and said to him: 'The Savior has been born.' But the angel didn't go where the king was but where the poor people were, which means that this message is not for the big shots but for the poor little guys, which means the oppressed, which means us."

I: "It was really the shepherds who were at the bottom of the social scale in Israel . . . "

ALEJANDRO: "And the good news is that

they're going to find somebody just like themselves, a poor guy wrapped in swaddling clothes."

*Today was born in the city of David
a Savior for you, who is Christ the Lord.*

FÉLIX: "He's making it clear that it's for them that he's coming. It seems to me that they were like slaves and when they heard that a liberator was coming they were filled with joy. They already knew that a Messiah was coming, and when they hear the angel announce that he's already here they're filled with joy. They know that this birth was going to free them from slavery, because, like the slaves that they were, they were forced to work. A liberator from all slavery. He was coming to liberate all slaves, all poor people, not just poor people of that time but those of today too! Every poor person who lives working for the rich lives like a slave."

FELIPE: "Every worker is always poor, even if he works in a factory."

FÉLIX goes on: "He was coming to liberate the poor. He wasn't coming to liberate the rich. That's why the news had to come to poor people. It was for them most of all. And it's the same now: The news, the word of God always goes to the poor people. Because I believe that the poor people, because of their poverty, always hear the word of God more often than the rich. A lot of rich people go to church on Sun-

53

.day but they don't listen to the word of God, they go to enjoy themselves . . . or they don't go."

SABINO: "It's the same with a lot of poor people here. . . . They don't come to church . . . "

FRANCISCO: "Even the angel didn't reach all the poor people . . . "

FELIPE: "The Gospel says he came to people who were working, not to people who were loafing."

FÉLIX: "Well, the Holy Spirit always comes more to poor people nowadays, because the poor people in their slavery have to turn to God every day. And when you least expect it, maybe working in the field, suddenly you get a good idea: That means the Spirit came to you."

ÓSCAR: "They were like us, poor and in need of a liberator. Because they took care of the animals, but on the other hand they were alone, abandoned by everybody. That's the way we are, humiliated by the rich too. But if somebody comes to tell us that we shouldn't be always serving those rich people like slaves, comes to talk to us about Revolution, something like that, then we gradually realize that we too can struggle."

JULIO: "It seems to me that we are the shepherds of the rich people because we work for them. We support them with our work, and a liberator has to come to help us too. We are *campesinos* and woodcutters, but it seems to

54

me that we don't need an angel to come to tell us personally. Or maybe he already came . . . "

FELIPE: "The angel is any idea, any inspiration that you get in the woods when you're there cutting wood, like Félix says, any idea about doing something for other people, for the community. It's the Holy Spirit, because the Spirit is the spirit of love for others, right?"

JULIO: "Well, that's why I just said that maybe that angel already came and we don't need to wait for him to come in the form of a vision, personally, because maybe right now when we're reading this and hearing these words the angel is coming to give us the news."

I: "That's right. At this very moment you are receiving the same news from the angel that the shepherds received."

LAUREANO: "We already got the news. But we have to do the work . . . "

"We have to spread the news," interrupted his cousin JULIO.

LAUREANO continued: "To find ways to liberate ourselves. Because liberation comes through people."

FELIPE: "Those who are against it, it's always because of selfishness."

ÓSCAR: "Also because of fear. A lot of us are afraid. Afraid that they'll do us some harm, prison, death. . . And a lot of times this fear is from ignorance."

And as a sign, you will find the baby
wrapped in swaddling clothes,
lying in a manger.

ÓSCAR: "He was born in a farmyard. He came for the sake of poor people, the liberator. That's why he had to be born like that. He had to set an example for us. That nobody should think he's better than others. To feel ourselves all the same, equal. Because everybody was born from the same womb, his mother's."

ÁNGEL, Félix's son: "If they'd been offered a good house wouldn't Mary and Joseph have accepted it?"

RAFAEL: "They wouldn't have turned it down, I bet."

ÓSCAR: "Then it would have been better if he hadn't come."

FÉLIX: "He was coming to let the poor know he was their comrade."

ÁNGEL: "The only reason they didn't accept a house is because nobody offered them one."

JULIO: "Why didn't anybody offer them one?"

ÓSCAR: "They were very poor. That's why."

TOMÁS PEÑA: "Maybe people thought they were slippery characters, that they were going to steal . . . "

FÉLIX: "That's what happens nowadays. If some raggedy people come to the city and ask for a place to stay they don't get any, or if they

56

do it'll be off in a chicken coop, to sleep with the chickens."

TOMÁS: "If he had been born in a rich man's house the shepherds wouldn't have been able to get there, because it was a fancy house. Maybe they wouldn't even have let them in."

ÓSCAR: "The shepherds wouldn't even have wanted to go there because they would have seen he wasn't coming for them but for the rich."

I said: "And the rich don't need liberation. What liberation do the rich need!"

WILLIAM: "The rich need to be liberated from their money."

FELIPE: "When the poor get liberated, they'll get liberated too."

Little ADÁN: "The poor will liberate them."

FRANCISCO: "And the poor also have the chance to be great, like the Messiah who was born like the common people."

I said: "The people really have great abilities that only need to be developed. When the people have education, enough food ... "

NATALIA: "Like in Cuba, where all the children are healthy. They're all taken care of when they're sick and everything. If you're old they take care of you. They give you everything you need and you're healthy and eager to work. And there the poor can learn a profession. And where can anybody do that here?"

And suddenly next to the angel
appeared many other angels from heaven
praising God, and saying,
"Glory to God in the highest;
and on earth peace to men who love."

Old TOMÁS PEÑA asked: "Those other angels who had stayed behind, who didn't come with the other angel, was it because God hadn't enlightened them yet, or was it because they had to come farther?"

I said: "Or because the shepherds hadn't seen them. First an angel speaks to them, afterwards they hear others ... "

TOMÁS: "It's like us here. We're all listening, but we don't manage to understand everything. So then, those who had heard hadn't taken it all in."

DON JULIO CHAVARRÍA: "Not until that moment was there peace on earth—when the child was born. And that's probably why there was joy in heaven. That's what the angels are singing, it seems to me."

EDGARD, a young man who had been a Franciscan and who was visiting us, said: "The glory of God can't exist in heaven until there is peace among men, which means justice, brotherhood, equality (peace is all this). The rich often believe that they give glory to God, but they don't give peace and justice, and so they don't give glory to God because the two things go together."

WILLIAM: "When there is peace, love, there is glory to God."

> *They went quickly and found Mary and*
>   *Joseph, and the child lying in the manger.*
> *When they saw him,*
> *they told what the angel had said to them*
>   *about the child,*
> *and all those who heard them*
> *wondered at what they said.*

JULIO: "Before they felt oppressed, and when the Savior came, they felt free and told about their joy."

TOMÁS: "And then all the people were happy, I mean the poor people, because the new news reached them all."

> *But Mary kept all this in her heart,*
> *thinking about it.*

TOMÁS: "She wasn't surprised like the rest of them, because she was lit up by the Holy Spirit and by everything that had happened to her. But even so she thought that maybe others would tell things that weren't so. They would make them bigger and say things they hadn't seen. And she also thought that they could kill him, or do something else to him, right? Dangerous . . . They could do all kinds of bad things to him."

I: "Yes, Mary already knew from the Annunciation that Jesus would be the Messiah . . . "

TOMÁS: "She thought they could hurt him because he was the Messiah. And they did attack him. Because since he was coming to liberate us, all the people, he would face many enemies. He was going to have many struggles."

JULIO: "And if Mary knew that's why Jesus was coming, and she knew it more sooner than the angels, why didn't she tell? Why did she wait for the angels to tell? It seems to me she was afraid they would come to kill him, so she'd rather keep the secret. That's why she didn't tell."

ÓSCAR: "The shepherds knew it. The king and the rich people didn't know it. The same thing happens now. Not everybody knows about the coming of this Jesus."

JULIO: "I think a lot of people know about it, but what happens is that there's a lot of fear. They don't dare approach like the shepherds did because they're afraid. And there are a lot of other people who don't know about it."

8.

The Visit of the Wise Men

(MATTHEW 2:1–12)

*Jesus was born in Bethlehem of Judea
in the days of Herod the King.
Then to Jerusalem came wise men
    from the East saying:
"Where is the King of the Jews
    that has been born?
For we saw his star in the East
and we have come here to worship him."*

We were in the church. I said by way of intro-
duction that these words of Matthew, "in the
days of Herod the King," are telling us that
Jesus was born under a tyranny. There were
three Herods, as we might say in Nicaragua
three Somozas: Herod the elder, Herod his
son, and a grandson Herod. Herod the elder,
the one at the time of Jesus' birth, had ordered
two of his sons to be strangled on suspicion of
conspiracy, and he also killed one of his wives.
At the time of Jesus' birth he killed more than

three hundred public servants on other suspicions of conspiracy. So Jesus was born in an atmosphere of repression and terror. It was known that the Messiah was going to be king, and that's why the wise men arrived asking for the king of the Jews, meaning the Messiah. The wise men were often priests and sometimes they became kings, but they were above all philosophers and people devoted to the study of the sciences, especially that of the stars. Perhaps they would be more like what we would call scientists than wise men. And they also taught a religious doctrine, that of Zoroaster. The star they speak of could have been a comet, like the comet Kohoutek now approaching the earth. (We know that at the time of Christ's birth there was a great one, now called Halley's comet.) Or it could have been any other celestial phenomenon, or it might have been only a way of speaking, peculiar to the Orient, comparing the Messiah with a star. Possibly this whole passage from Matthew is fiction, an imaginary narrative that he chose to insert here. But it could have happened this way."

LAUREANO said: "I think these wise men shit things up when they went to Herod asking about a liberator. It would be like someone going to Somoza now to ask him where's the man who's going to liberate Nicaragua."

Another of the young men: "The way I figure it, these wise men were afraid of Herod and didn't want to do anything without his consent."

TOMÁS PEÑA: "They went to ask him for a pass ... "

The same young man: "They probably went first to consult Herod because they were afraid of him, and all those people of Jerusalem were filled with fear when they heard talk of a Messiah, just like Nicaraguan people are afraid when they hear talk of liberation. The minute they hear that young people want to liberate those of us who are being exploited, they begin to shake and be afraid. When they hear people say that this government must be overthrown, they shake and are afraid."

ADÁN: "It seems to me that when those wise men arrived they knew that the Messiah had been born and they thought Herod knew about it and that the Messiah was going to be a member of his family. If he was a king, it was natural that they should go to look for him in Herod's palace. But in that palace there was nothing but corruption and evil, and the Messiah couldn't be born there. He had to be born among the people, poor, in a stable. They learned a lesson there when they saw that the Messiah had not been born in a palace or in the home of some rich person, and that's why they had to go on looking for him somewhere else. The Gospel says later that when they left there they saw the star again. That means

63

that when they reached Jerusalem the star wasn't guiding them. They'd lost it."

FÉLIX: "They were confused. And it seems to me that since they were foreigners they didn't know the country very well, and they went to the capital, where the authorities were, to ask about the new leader."

When Herod the king heard this
he was very troubled,
and all the people of Jerusalem also.

ÓSCAR: "I figure that when Herod found out that that king had been born he was furious because he didn't want to stop being the ruler. He was as mad as hell. And he was already figuring out how to get rid of this one like he had got rid of so many already."

PABLO: "He must have felt hatred and envy. Because dictators always think they are gods. They think they're the only ones and they can't let anyone be above them."

GLORIA: "And he was probably afraid, too. He had killed a lot of people not long before, and then some gentlemen arrive asking where's the new king, the liberator."

FÉLIX: "He surely must have put all his police on the alert. I think that's what the Gospel means here: 'He was very troubled.' "

One of the young people: "And the Gospel says that the other people of Jerusalem were also troubled. That means his followers, the big shots, like the Somoza crowd. Because for them it was very bad news that the liberator was arriving. But for poor people it was great news. And the powerful people knew that the Messiah had to be against them."

Old TOMÁS PEÑA: "That king who ruled that republic with a firm hand—he ruled a million people or however many there were then—he didn't allow anyone to say anything he didn't like. You could only think the way the government wanted, and they surely didn't allow any talk about messiahs. And they must have been annoyed when outsiders came talking about that, as if they were talking about a new government."

MANUEL: "The people had been waiting for that Messiah or liberator for some time. And it's interesting to see that even out of the country the news had got around that he had been born, and these wise men found out, it seems to me, from the people. But in Jerusalem the powerful were entirely ignorant of his birth."

Then the king called
*   all the chiefs of the priests*
and those who taught the law to the people,
and he asked them where Christ
*   was going to be born.*

FELIPE: "The clergy are summoned by a tyrant who has killed a lot of people. And the clergy answer the call. It seems to me that if they went to his palace it's because they were his supporters, they approved of his murders.

Just like today the monsignors who are supporters of the regime that we have. It means that those people were like the people we have today in Nicaragua."

They told him: "In Bethlehem of Judea:
for thus it is written by the prophet."

I said that they knew the Bible well and that they knew that the Messiah was to be born in that little town called Bethlehem.

DON JOSÉ: "They knew he was going to be born in a little town, among the common people. But they were in Jerusalem, visiting with the powerful and the rich in their palaces. Just like today there are a lot of Church leaders who know that Jesus was born in Bethlehem, and every year they preach about this at Christmas, that Jesus was born poor in a manger, but the places they go to all the time are rich people's houses and palaces."

Then Herod summoned the wise men
in secret and asked them the exact time
when the star had appeared.
Then he sent them to Bethlehem, and said,
"Go and find out about that child
and when you find him, let me know,
so that I may go and worship him also."

REBECA: "Herod hears he's going to be born in a little town, like you might say here in Solentiname, which isn't much. That's why he asks the wise men to let him know when they've found the child. Because how else is he going to find out about the Messiah if the Messiah is born among the people, a poor woman's little kid. The people around there in those parts, they would know about it, but they'd keep it a secret."

When they saw the star again
they were filled with joy.
They went into the house;
they saw the child with Mary his mother,
and they knelt down and worshipped him.
Then they opened their boxes
and they gave him presents of gold,
    incense, and myrrh.

TOMÁS: "They come and open their presents —some perfumes and a few things of gold. It doesn't seem as if he got big presents. Because those foreigners that could have brought him a big sack of gold, a whole bunch of coins, or maybe bills, they didn't bring these things. What they brought to him were little things. . . . That's the way we ought to go, poor, humble, the way we are. At least that's what I think."

OLIVIA: "It's on account of these gifts from the wise men that the rich have the custom of giving presents at Christmas. But they give them to each other."

MARCELINO: "The stores are full of Christmas presents in the cities, and they make lots of money. But it's not the festival of the birth of the child Jesus. It's the festival of the birth of the son of King Herod."

Afterwards, being warned in a dream
that they should not return
* to where Herod was,*
they returned to their country
* by another way.*

TOMÁS: "The wise men go off by another route. He inspired them not to inform on him, because he was already a fugitive. He made them see they shouldn't go back the same way. It was better to go another way. Already defending his body. At least that's what I think."

FELIPE: "By now they were like fugitives too. They went off by another way like they were fleeing. And I think that if they'd returned to the capital they'd have been killed."

ALEJANDRO: "Well, the liberator was born in an atmosphere of persecution, and those who come to see him are also persecuted. The people must have kept the secret . . . "

OLIVIA, his mother: "The truth is that ever since he was at his mother's breast he had the rich against him. When she was pregnant Mary had sung that her son was coming to dethrone the powerful and to heap good things upon the poor and to leave the rich without a single thing. And from his birth they pursued him to kill him, and then he had to flee in his mother's arms and with his papa . . . "

GLORIA: "Those common people had a hope now. And as soon as they found out he'd been born they felt happy. The neighbors all knew.

That star, maybe it was the townspeople talking, and it got to the wise men."

TOMÁS, with his great simplicity: "This comes down pretty much to what I said before, maybe not quite, but more or less: We heard that a priest was coming here. Then we believed it and we said, 'If a priest is coming to Solentiname it'll be a great thing. We're going to live happier, better, or in some other way.' It seems that the whole town was glad because the place was going to have a priest. Well that's the way I think it was at that time. They had to be glad because of the birth of this little kid . . . "

CHAEL: "Those wise gentlemen found something they weren't expecting—that the liberator was a poor little child, and besides, a little child persecuted by the powerful."

LAUREANO: "The ones who were persecuting him were the rulers. He was a guy that was coming to change everything, coming to make everybody equal, coming to liberate the poor and to take power away from the rulers because they were shitting everything up. And that's why the powerful went after him to kill him."

9.

The Slaughter of the Innocents

(MATTHEW 2:12–23)

Shortly before we had Mass this Sunday a National Guard patrol came to inspect our houses. (Martial law had been declared throughout the country, with a suspension of individual liberties.) Some people seemed to be a little afraid, but the children rushed gaily throughout the church and made so much noise that it was hard at times for us to hear clearly the commentaries on this Gospel passage. MYRIAM had read:

> *After the wise men left,*
> *an angel of the Lord appeared to Joseph*
> *in his sleep and said to him:*
> *"Get up, take the child and his mother,*
> *and flee to the land of Egypt*
> *and stay there until I tell you to come back.*
> *Because Herod is going to look*
> *for the child to kill him."*

Among those present was my brother FERNANDO (a Jesuit priest), and he said: "I think that if Mary, when she was waiting for the birth of the infant, had the idea of a messiah who would be in power, she quickly lost the idea. She realized that she had given birth to a messiah who was subversive from birth. And I also think that for a long time we have been misreading the Gospel, interpreting in a purely spiritual sense, eliminating all its political and social circumstances, which are certainly very dramatic; that is, we have abstracted the Gospel from its reality. How often have I read that Saint Joseph and the Virgin fled to Egypt. But only now, when an army patrol has just come, have I really understood that very real and harsh circumstance that the Gospel presents to us here: repression. We can imagine what this means: leaving at night, hiding, with great fear, leaving everything behind, and having to reach the border because they are being pursued."

One of the ladies said: "It's very rough, but what happened then has gone on in every age. There was a king like those who exist now in many countries, in our country and in many others, and if that child was coming to liberate from injustice, the ruler had to pursue him and try to kill him so that the people would live forever in slavery. The same thing happens here the minute a good person appears. We've seen how in the north they've killed that union leader Catalino Flores. I heard the news on the Cuban radio; up to then I still thought it wasn't true. Sure, they always persecute people who want to free the rest, and they kill them. That's what happened to Jesus; they tried to eliminate him when he was a child."

Another of the ladies: "Yes, that's just like what goes on nowadays, and it's because anyone that is struggling for the liberation of the oppressed, he himself is a Christ, and then there's a Herod, and what we're seeing is the living story of the life of Jesus. And more Herods will come along, because whenever there's someone struggling for liberation there's someone who wants to kill him, and if they can kill him they will. How happy Somoza would have been if Ernesto and Fernando had died when they were little kids so they wouldn't be teaching all this. It's perfectly clear that the business of Herod and Christ, we have it right here."

One of the boys: "I think that the same thing happened to Catalino Flores as to Christ, exactly. They didn't kill him when he was a child because he, like Jesus, managed to escape. They killed him at an age when he had already fought his fight. He fought, and they killed him, but the same thing happened to him as to Christ, that he is resurrected and is in the hearts of everyone that wants the things that he wanted."

DONALD, who is studying in a small town on the Costa Rican border and has come home for his vacation: "But in the Gospel it's a tiny child that they're persecuting, and here they're not going to persecute a newborn child. From the time he was born, they were looking for Jesus to kill him, and his parents had to save his life."

Another of the boys: "I think the same thing happens here, Donald. Can I say something? You know what country we're in, and how there's so much infant mortality, and so many stunted, undernourished children. I think that's persecuting children. I think the same thing is happening here as happened to Christ when he was persecuted as a kid."

And I said that there are many *campesino* families that have had to leave their homes in many parts of Nicaragua, fleeing from misery and hunger, or because they have been driven off their lands, or because the National Guard is killing the *campesino* leaders, burning farmhouses, raping women, jailing whole families, torturing. And the picture of all those families fleeing, mothers carrying their children in their arms, is the same as the flight to Egypt.

LAUREANO: "Another thing: The revolutionary conscience in these countries is still a child. It's still tiny. And they persecute it so that it won't grow."

When Herod understood
that the wise men had tricked him
he got very furious
and he ordered the slaughter
of every child two years or under
who lived in and around Bethlehem.

A girl said: "The same thing happened up north when Catalino appeared: Since they

73

didn't know him well or even which one he was, they killed all the farmers around there."

Old TOMÁS PEÑA: "Herod ordered the kids killed since he wanted to reign forever and didn't want a liberator. Of course, when he heard 'There is a king' he said: 'There's no king but me. I better kill him.' And then he tried to figure how to kill him, but as Jesus Christ was more powerful than he was, he couldn't kill him."

Young ÓSCAR: "That Herod was a coward. It was because he was a coward that he committed all those murders. A lousy coward."

Young ALEJANDRO: "It's the same thing nowadays: As soon as they see the first signs of anything new, they get scared and begin to murder, as happened with this child. It's because these people are cowards, and it's cowardice that makes them kill defenseless people. Like Herod who didn't kill armed soldiers but poor children."

A Protestant who has come from the coast opposite: "They persecuted Jesus, but he wasn't in opposition to any government."

FELIPE: "He came as the king of the Jews. What more opposition do you want?"

Another young man: "Herod, of course, that millionaire, with his power he had everybody crushed. And the same thing happens here and in other places, wherever they're screwing the people. The innocent. Because the ones they're killing are the innocent, the ones who are dying, like that boy in the mountains up north. In all these cases they're killing the child that they don't want to see grow up. Back then something like that occurred. Herod was the Somoza of that region, and when he heard that that child had been born, he went after all the children. As soon as they glimpse a sprig of liberation anywhere, they do what Herod did."

LAUREANO: "And not only that, because Herod killed them after they were born; now they kill them before they're born with their famous Family Planning; they kill the children before they're born for fear that later there'll be a people that they won't be able to control."

I said that was very true, and that there are clinics set up all through the country where they sterilize women without their consent. This is a campaign that the United States is waging throughout Latin America. They have population experts throughout Latin America, in charge of seeing that the population doesn't increase. President Johnson once said in a speech that bringing up a Latin American cost the United States two hundred dollars, while stopping him from being born cost only five dollars. And as an economist has said: If births decrease, funds for investment will increase.

Another young man: "Herod was less cruel than these people."

WILLIAM: "That government was also set up by the Empire."

I said that in fact Herod had been put in power by the Roman intervention, and Rome allowed him to call himself "king," although he had very little power. I said also that this slaughter of the innocents, although it seems unlikely, was not so in the case of Herod, who slaughtered many families, and even his own children and his favorite wife. An historian of the period says that his anger was boundless. And it is said that he tried to arrange that on the day of his death children would be slaughtered in Jerusalem so that there would be a lot of mourning. The slaughter of children in a village, that could have been like our little town of Belén, in Rivas, or like Colón, or San Miguelito (and where there were probably not many children), it wouldn't be a cruelty very worthy of attention for historians, especially if Herod was involved. But those children under two years of age in that village (there might have been twenty of them) represent all the innocents that have died for the cause of Jesus, that is, for liberation, in the whole world.

In this way was fulfilled
   what was written
by the prophet Jeremiah:
"A voice was heard in Ramah,
weeping and great lamentation;
it is Rachel who weeps for her children,
and she will not be comforted
for they are dead."

LAUREANO: "I remember what happened in Chile, where they killed thousands of people, just because freedom was being born there; many people were taken up in airplanes and thrown out into the sea. But they can't put freedom down, just as Herod couldn't put Jesus down."

FELIPE: "And as I see it, Ernesto, we are taught here that to be powerful it isn't necessary to have money, because Christ was born very poor (Herod could not distinguish him from the other children of that village) and Christ was very powerful, so powerful that they were afraid, and they tried to kill him, and afterwards they did kill him but after his death he is even more powerful. So we are taught that we, even though we're very poor, must not feel humiliated, unfit, as they say, as though we had no right to live."

ELVIS: "The importance of the birth of Christ is that it was the birth of the Revolution, right? There are many people who are afraid of the word as they were afraid of Christ because he was coming to change the world. From then on the Revolution has been growing. It keeps growing little by little, then, and it keeps growing, and nobody can stop it."

I: "And it has to grow here also, doesn't it?"

PANCHO: "We have to get rid of selfishness and do what Christ said and go on with the Revolution, as you socialists say. I'm not a socialist, I'm not a revolutionary. I like to hear the talk and grasp what I can but really I'm nothing.

Although I *would* like to see a change in Nicaragua."

MANUEL: "But if there's going to be a change you have to cooperate with it, you've got to cooperate."

PANCHO: "But how do you do it! I'd like somebody to tell me: 'That's the way it's going to be done.' But you can't! When we rise up they kill us."

ALEJANDRO: "But look, they killed him too."

PANCHO: "Correct, but he was Christ and we're never going to compare ourselves with him."

MANUEL: "But I heard there have been other men, like Che, who also have died for freedom."

PANCHO: "Right. You can die, you, and tomorrow we'll all be dancing and we'll never think that you died for us."

WILLIAM: "Then you think that those deaths are useless?"

PANCHO: "They're useless. Or they're almost useless!"

Young MYRIAM: "I say that when there's someone who will free our country there will be another Christ."

My brother FERNANDO (to Pancho): "When you say 'What can I do? Nothing!' I agree with you. But when you ask another 'What can *we*

78

do?' I would say everything. And that day when you ask each other 'What do we do?' you'll already know what you are going to do. And the people all united are the same Jesus that you see in this manger scene, against whom Herod couldn't do a thing." (Fernando pointed to the clay manger scene, made by Mariíta, that we had put at the foot of the altar during this Christmas season.)

A young man from Solentiname who now lives elsewhere but who occasionally comes back: "I who have been away notice that the child is being born in this community. And I see the difference between this and the people that live in other places up in the mountains. Of course, up in the mountains it's different. If I sing a song there, they tell me I'm a communist. The way it is up there where we are, if anybody says anything against the government, they say: 'Go and find out who the communist is so they can come for him.' "

And his brother, who lives in Solentiname: "Ernesto, I'm going to tell you now about my brother. My brother, he knows what a Nativity scene is. We're brothers, after all. I'm going to say a little more. Since he went away, he always has the idea of clearing his conscience, he talks and talks there. Many farmers say, 'communist!' and they don't know what a communist is. Now he talks to them a lot, because he's told me, he talks up there to the young people. My brother has told me that some of them agree with him, others don't. He says he's not making much progress. I tell him: Don't be afraid, say what you know, even if it's only a little, I tell him, I know you'll get to them."

NATALIA, who is a midwife and has been present at the birth of so many children in Solentiname, said: "Well, as I see it, the birth of the child Jesus is also all of us, this unity that we have here. Because in ourselves we are seeing things clearly. But we must all help with this birth of Christ. Like when a baby is being born, and maybe you don't know anything, and they say to you: Come help me. Well, you go, not because you know anything, you don't know anything, right? But because a poor child is being born. See, I grabbed my petticoat, or if I have on my apron I put it on him! Because he's being born in need."

I: "That must be difficult, the birth of a child . . ."

NATALIA: "Oh yes, of course it is. Horrible, isn't it, terrible to see yourself in a fix like that, and maybe you want to know more, know something more, and you see the fix that your friend is in. But you tell her (even though you're dying), 'Don't worry!' Even though I was trembling, if my friend was trembling, I said, 'Don't worry. Don't worry, you'll be okay.' And you see the problem, and you're covered with cold sweat. This has happened to me. A friend calls me because maybe she thinks I know, and I don't know anything, or nothing more than what her faith puts into me, something."

ÓSCAR: "Ernesto, I want to say something. Do you know how I understand birth as I'm listening to Natalia? Very important, the birth of a child and even more to raise a child (I feel this deeply as the father of a family), but that's not the birth that this Gospel is telling us about. Do you know what I understand by a child here? It's the poor people! They are children with respect to the rich. I mean that we, then, since we're poor, we're children, we're always beneath the rich, and we feel maybe: 'I'd like to be like that one who's taking it easy over there.' Enjoying what I'd like to enjoy, and I can't, because they don't let me, understand? It seems to me, then, that's what this birth means, a little child who suffers. We ourselves, even though we're adults, are like children: the poor. But I say, the child is not always going to be tiny. I say to my brothers, my comrades: Hell, they're screwing us! We're giving them everything we have! Let's fight! That's what Christ did. He suffered, but he conquered. It's true that he died, as they say, on the cross, but for me he didn't die. And he's talking to us in parables; I understand them, so I'm relying on that. I think what he's telling us is to fight and establish justice. We ourselves are going to give justice to the earth, we the children, to those who are imposing injustice on us. Don't you believe that the child is always going to be crushed and hungry. I mean that the birth that the Scripture tells us about here is not like the birth of one of these kids romping around in the church. No, this child is me, you, everybody. But the rich have always tried to crush us like we crush the snake, by the head, wham!"

ALEJANDRO: "And as I see it that Jesus who was born in a manger, like a child is born here in the mountains, in a farmhouse or in a boat, is the liberation that's also being born here, in a humble form. And even in those kids who are still so young, who are playing there, and who have been born like this, inside them, even though they don't know it, something is being born: freedom."

Another young man: "They're learning. The child laughs and makes noise and racket, but inside him freedom is being born."

After a pause: "Since I was a small boy I've realized that. I don't know anything about politics. I don't know anything about other things either. I'm not a reader or anything. I understand all right but I can't express myself. It bothers me and I want to express myself but I can't. Some people tell me I ought to be happy with this regime because we haven't had wars. You're a young man, they say, and since you were born you've never seen a war and you don't even know what war is. Hell, I say to them, I don't know about those wars, but do you know what war is for me? Hunger, I tell them, because I've suffered hunger, I tell them, together with my mother; one time I even ate salt, I tell them, just salt, I tell them."

Afterwards we read how Joseph was informed by an angel of the death of Herod and he returned to Israel:

> *But when Joseph learned*
> *that Archelaus was governing in Judea*
> *in place of his father Herod,*
> *he was afraid to go there;*
> *and having been warned in dreams,*
> *he went to the province of Galilee.*
> *When he reached there,*
> *he went to live in the town of Nazareth.*

WILLIAM: "They were practically in the underground."

Another boy: "They were right to stay in hiding, because even if Herod was already dead, there was another dictator there; just as if a Somoza dies and somebody else is in power, you're still always afraid."

I said that this Herod Archelaus that was left governing Judea was the cruelest of the sons of Herod and was even crueler than his father; his government was inaugurated with a riot by the people and he killed more than three thousand demonstrators who were asking for freedom for political prisoners and for tax cuts. In Galilee Herod Antipas ruled, who was less dreadful, even though he was the one that killed John the Baptist and was governing at the time of the death of Christ.

My brother FERNANDO said: "The old dictator

83

died and the angel tells Joseph that they can come back now, but that doesn't mean that now there wouldn't be more people that would want to kill the child. In fact his life continued in danger and that's why they went to that insignificant little town of Galilee, and part of his public life he also spent half in hiding, until they finally killed him. And the same thing will happen to anyone who gets involved with liberation: He'll get out of one danger only to fall into another. And this you always have to keep in mind. The angel informed them only that one danger had ended ... for the moment."

ALEJANDRO: "And Mary was screwed from the very first, right? It was thirty years of fighting right beside her son, risking herself just like him, from when he was a child until he died. That seems to me a good lesson for every mother. And another lesson was Joseph."

And OLIVIA, Alejandro's mother: "What Alejandro says is quite right, and fathers and mothers ought to think a lot about it. That mother went with her son until his death and willingly. But nowadays many times mothers are the first to be opposed to their sons fighting for freedom. Some of them don't even like the boys and girls to come to the meetings, so they don't get involved. I, when I heard that some young people were taking over at the cathedral, I wanted to be close to them, I wanted to be able to go and see them, help

84

them in some way. And even take the microphone and talk also."

FERNANDO: "I don't understand how you can read the Gospels and get spiritual lessons for your life out of it and not get involved in the Revolution. This Book has a very clear political position for anyone that reads it simply, as you read it. But there are people in Managua who read this Book, and they are friends of Herod; and they don't realize that this Book is their enemy."

So that what the prophets said
  could be fulfilled:
that Jesus was going to be
  called a Nazarene.

I said that Nazareth was a place so humble that it is not mentioned even once in the Old Testament, and we do not know exactly what prophecies Saint Matthew is referring to. It is believed that he may be punning with a Hebrew name of similar sound that had been given to the Messiah and that means "sprout." One thing seems certain, and that is that the name "Nazarene" that Jesus had was a nickname given him by his enemies to make fun of his humble origin.

GLORIA: "To say 'from Nazareth' might be like saying 'from Nindirí' . . . or worse, 'from Solentiname.' "

JOSÉ, Mariíta's husband, said: "His nickname meant that he was a man of the people, and he *was* a man of the people, including even that his parents hadn't been married, were engaged to be married and she was pregnant, as often happens with the poor; with that problem of the poor, then, the Messiah was born, son of an unwed mother."

WILLIAM (smiling): "And they didn't know who the father was ... "

MARIÍTA: "But he married her because he loved her."

10.

The Child Jesus and Old Simeon

(LUKE 2:29–36)

We read the story of how old Simeon, who was waiting for the liberation of Israel, went to the temple guided by the Holy Spirit, and when he saw the child he took him up in his arms and prophesied upon him. We commented on Simeon's first words:

Lord, now you can let me die in peace,
because you have fulfilled
what you promised to your servant.

WILLIAM: "That little old Simeon was speaking in the name of the whole community. We can die in peace because he has come, he has finally come, the one we've been waiting for. It's the relief of the whole community that finally gets to see what it had been expecting for so long. All of humanity was waiting for him. It's all humanity that says, 'He has finally come.' "

TOMÁS PEÑA: "A great joy for him, it appears,

because he finally came, and Simeon needed that coming to be able to die, like a rest that he was going to have in death."

His son, FELIPE: "This gives me an idea, Ernesto: Before the liberator was born people died without joy, without hope. They died thinking about what they didn't even know, right? But when this man dies he knows that the liberator is on earth, and that all the other people won't die hopeless."

WILLIAM: "Yes, what Felipe says is very true. Because if you read the Old Testament, when they speak of death, the kings, the wise men, and the prophets, they always do so with a lot of pain. Because they're going to go down to Sheol, and they beg the Lord not to let them die yet. Because they saw everything as a great darkness. They didn't know what was on the other side. And this little old man, what a contrast: He's going to die happy. Not only because he's seen the savior with his own eyes but because he knows what's coming after."

TERESITA: "He also is coming to conquer death . . . "

With my eyes I have seen the Savior,
that you have placed before all the people.

FELIPE: "He says he's for everybody. The liberator is for everybody, but some follow him and others don't. In fact, he's not for everybody but only for the ones who want to follow him. He could be for everybody if everybody wanted to follow him."

TOMÁS: "Of course. He's for the ones who want to follow him. Those are the ones mentioned here."

WILLIAM: "As a leader, as a chief. The one who goes ahead."

He is the light that is to lighten those who are not the people of Israel.

ALEJANDRO: "I think he's for everyone, not just for the ones who want to follow him. It seems to me that everybody should receive this light someday, even though just then it was only that little old man. But he understood that the light was not just for him. And he says for those who are not of Israel. He means he's for everybody, not just for Israel. I understand that everybody is called, right?"

FELIPE: "No, Alejandro, nobody said it wasn't this way. We said that Jesus Christ came for everybody but not everybody wants to follow him. But he did come for everybody."

WILLIAM: "He's a light that's put out in front and everybody sees it, and anybody who wants to follow follows . . . "

FELIPE: "Sure, everybody has the light, but if somebody wants to stay in the darkness, well . . . "

ALEJANDRO: "No, that's why he's the light, so he can reach everybody."

DON PATRICIO: "Some people don't want to see . . . "

CHAEL: "That's not his fault, the one who's the light."

NATALIA, Chael's mother: "Anybody who wants to follow the light should follow it, because he'll be lit up by the light. It's the way we follow you. You're giving us instruction. And if we don't want to follow you it must be out of fear, fright. Stupidity. Because Christ wasn't afraid when he was making his Revolution! Well, that's the way we ought to be. Because maybe they'll put us in jail, because maybe they'll . . . ! We have to die! 'I'm not going to get into that,' 'I don't want anything to happen to me,' 'I'm staying out of that . . . ' No! 'I'm going and if they're going to kill me, well, let them kill me, and if they're going to throw me in jail, I'm going.' "

JULIO: "Get out in front, right?"

FELIPE: "That business of wanting to save your body and lose your soul . . . "

"We have to leave fear behind us," NATALIA said again.

I said to them: "The light that the Gospel talks about is the one that Natalia is transmitting to us. Her words are enlightening us for action."

And to give honor to Israel your people.

ALEJANDRO: "He says he has come to enlighten those who are not of Israel. Israel is the chosen people, the one that goes ahead, the leaders, and that's why the coming of the Messiah is an honor for Israel. But in reality the liberation is for everybody, for the whole world."

I said that a few verses before it says that the little old man was waiting for the liberation of Israel. Now with the child in his arms he says that the liberation of Israel is for all peoples.

JULIO: "Israel was a poor and marginal people and he came to liberate them. It was like a poor neighborhood, like you could say Acahualinca in Managua. But a liberator who came to liberate the people in those neighborhoods would afterwards come to liberate the whole Nicaraguan people, not just those poor neighborhoods."

I: "Through those poor people he would liberate the others. Those poor people would be the liberation of the others. . . . It was the same way with Israel. God chose that oppressed people and decided to liberate them and by means of them to liberate the other peoples of the earth."

WILLIAM: "That's the way it was in Cuba. The liberation of that people will go on to become the liberation of all the other peoples."

Joseph and the mother of Jesus
were surprised by what Simeon
was saying of the child.

"Were surprised," I said, "means that they understood all that we're understanding now."

Then Simeon blessed them,
and he said to Mary, the mother of Jesus:
"This child is destined to make many in
Israel fall or rise up."

ELVIS, another of Natalia's sons: "The ones who are going to fall are the rich, and the poor are going to rise up, right?"

FELIPE: "The bandits, the bad people were the ones who were going to fall. The good ones are the ones who are going to rise up. The exploiters fall when the poor people don't obey them anymore and rise up."

TERESITA: "What Mary announced in the Magnificat is going to be fulfilled, that the proud shall be humbled and the humble raised up."

MARCELINO: "From that time on, the world has been getting freer, don't you think, Father? It's not so bad as in the old days when those kings had slaves."

I said that in fact the human condition in history had gradually improved through changes and revolutions.

TOMÁS PEÑA said: "And now the rich are offering more wages, so that the poor can live a little better. Before, when you came for a job there was a huge number of workers and so they only gave you a little. And the work was very hard."

I said that the situation had improved somewhat but that only with a total change, with a

Revolution, could things be set right once and for all.

TOMÁS: "But maybe little by little . . . "

FELIPE: "Ernesto, it seems to me that what my papa said, that the rich are giving us a little more pay, they're doing this to keep the people distracted, deceived, so that they won't rebel. It's a tactic they're using so the people won't rebel. But we have to be careful. Just because they pay us a little more doesn't mean that we're going to put up with them forever."

WILLIAM, smiling: "The Alliance for Progress?"

CHAEL: "It loosens the noose a little . . . "

TOMÁS: "Yes, that's what they're doing, little by little, it seems to me. Because instead of the way they used to be, they're a little looser. But it's clear we'd like to have things change once and for all. But since they can't, we just have to go on struggling."

> *He will be a sign that many will reject,*
> *and it will be known*
> *what each one thinks in his heart.*
> *But for you all this will be like a sword*
> *that will pierce your heart.*

REBECA: "They were Mary's sufferings when they were persecuting him and when they took him off to be killed, all tied up, and all that, and they were beating him. Those were the sufferings that she had in her heart."

WILLIAM: "That's what you can't get around in

the process of liberation: grief. You've always got to keep it in mind. That's the way it just has to be."

FELIPE: "That's what happened to Jesus and it keeps on happening to anybody who tries to liberate the people."

WILLIAM: "It keeps on happening."

I said that's why Mary has traditionally been pictured with a sword in her heart. Her grief was because many people would reject her son ("a sign that many will reject") and because with the coming of her son the divisions in humanity would be evident ("what each one thinks in his heart"). This is the same thing we now call class distinctions. And it was these distinctions which divide humanity that caused the passion and death of Jesus and are still like a sword that breaks Mary's heart in two.

11.

The Child Jesus in the Temple

(LUKE 2:41–52)

When Jesus was twelve years old
they all went to Jerusalem
as was the custom of that feast.
And when they returned,
after the feast was ended,
the child Jesus stayed behind in Jerusalem;
and Joseph and his mother did not know this.

The young people began to talk. First MANUEL: "He disobeyed. He gave them the slip. And young people should disobey when their parents want to keep them just for themselves, when they want to take them away from the community, from their work with other young people, from their duty, from the struggle."

Afterwards, LAUREANO, who always talks of Revolution: "Like the guerrilla fighters who go off to fight against the wishes of their parents."

And one of the old men: "Was it right for a child of twelve to do that? Shouldn't he have asked permission first? They wouldn't have refused it. Imagine how worried they felt as they went around looking for him. Mary scolded him . . . "

And another one of the young people: "Maybe they wouldn't have given him permission. And that's why he had to do it that way. Jesus here gives us a lesson about independence from the family."

OLIVIA: "He also did it to help prepare them. He was going to be away from them later. And once Mary and his other relatives came looking for him, and he told them that his family was the community. And then Mary lost him in death, but on the third day, like here in the temple, he was found."

Three days later
they found him in the temple,
sitting in the midst of the teachers
* of the law,*
listening to them and asking them
* questions.*
And all who heard him were astonished
* at his intelligence*
and at the answers that he gave.

MANUEL: "He asked questions and gave answers. It was to conscientize them."

OLIVIA: "He went to the temple to teach the teachers of the law, because these teachers knew the law by heart but they didn't put it into practice."

ALEJANDRO: "And he chose the temple because it was the center of their religion. He went right to the root of it. Because since religion was corrupt, he wanted to attack the evil at the root, in the temple and with the leaders."

FELIPE added: "In this Gospel Jesus appears as a rebellious kid. He's still a child and he's already in the temple challenging their religion, criticizing and arguing with those guys, giving them arguments they can't answer."

MANUEL: "He talked to the doctors because the young always have something new to say to the old. Something that the old don't know. Only young people can say these things, I say."

And I said then that what they had said had shed a lot of light on this for me. Now I saw it clearly: Jesus was taken to the temple by his parents, in accordance with the religious traditions that they faithfully observed, "as was the custom," as the Gospel says. There he saw the Jewish religion, legalistic, pharisaical, external. He also saw the money-changers that he was going to drive out later. And then, when his parents were leaving, he went back to the temple to see if he could do something to change the situation.

WILLIAM: "I see in this a lesson for young people. They have to take an interest in correcting their religion when they see that it's evil, ruined by old people. Talk to them, tell them the way Jesus told the teachers of the law: 'You stupid bastards, that's not the way to do it. . . . ' They took him to the temple to fulfill a ritual like all the Jews, but here he committed his first act of rebellion. . . . First, at that age, he criticizes the temple (questioning the priests). Then he attacks the temple (when he drove out the merchants). Then he declares that there shouldn't even be a temple anymore. The only temple for him is the unity of all people."

FELIPE: "Conclusion, then: Jesus was a revolutionary from childhood."

When his parents saw him,
they were amazed:
and his mother said to him,
"My son, why have you done this to us?
Your father and I have been very worried,
*   looking for you."*
He said to them,
"Why were you looking for me?
Don't you know that I have to be
*   about my Father's business?"*
But they did not understand
what he said to them.

ALEJANDRO: "What didn't they understand? That he had to attend to his Father's business they sure understood. What they didn't understand, it seems to me, is that he had to challenge their religion, and that was his Father's business."

OLIVIA: "I think that Mary was already afraid. When he slipped away she must have thought that he had probably escaped to start the liberation. That's why he says to them: 'Why did you look for me if you knew that I have to devote myself to these affairs?' His Father's affairs were to bring liberation. It's clear that Mary probably didn't understand everything and still had a lot to learn. The son would gradually conscientize them."

Then he returned with them to Nazareth
and went on being obedient to them.
And his mother kept all this in her heart.

PABLO: "It says he went on being obedient to them, so he hadn't been disobedient. Because to obey God was not to disobey them, even though he had slipped away from them."

REBECA: "Mary accepted the attitude of Jesus. That's what it means when it says that she kept those things in her heart. And she meditated about it. She probably didn't understand everything at the beginning. She was a humble woman, without education. But she would gradually understand everything in time."

TOMÁS: "And almost surely she was wondering when would be the next time he would get in trouble."

Meanwhile Jesus went on growing
in body and mind,
and he had the approval of God
and of all the people.

FÉLIX: "He was developing in love. That was

his growing up. He was maturing in his love for people."

ÓSCAR: "And he didn't just grow once. He grows and develops in a community every time that love and unity among everyone in the community develop and grow. And so now here among us Jesus is growing. He is developing and becoming a man."

12.

John the Baptist in the Desert

(LUKE 3:1–20)

At that time God spoke to John,
the son of Zacharias, in the wilderness.
And he passed through all the places
near the River Jordan,
telling people that they ought to change
their attitudes and be baptized,
so that their sins could be forgiven.

TOMÁS: "It seems to me that nobody there was baptized, right? He was coming to baptize them, it seems to me, so that they would change their attitude and look for the straight path and not look for the crooked path. The water wouldn't do it. They had to change their attitude."

OLIVIA: "It's a lesson for us because we're all baptized and yet even now every one of us is full of selfishness. The one who has most and is rich doesn't want to share his riches with the rest. He doesn't want to give—not even to pay what's fair, much less to give. So the baptism we have is just a baptism of water, not a change of attitude. The rich are the first to get baptized, as soon as they're born. They do this because they have money and there's a big party with delicious food and they drink toasts."

FÉLIX: "The rich child is baptized as soon as he's born, but the baby has no understanding or knowledge. He doesn't know anything, and the baby who's not baptized is just the same, you see? God sent John the Baptist to baptize those Christians because they were people of understanding and John the Baptist was telling them what they had to do. And they had to understand. But not now. A child is baptized, and he's just the same. And his father has little interest in showing him the road to God. And if nobody shows him the way he stays the same, he never knows anything. But his father ought to show him the road to God, and that's what God told John to show them . . . "

Someone said: "And John was the first one to change his attitude."

Another: "It seems to me that he didn't change his attitude. He was close to God ever since he was born."

TERE (holding her son Juan in her arms): "It's interesting to see that he, a *campesino*, was sent to baptize and conscientize, and not a priest."

This happened just as the prophet Isaiah
* had written:*
"The voice is heard of someone
* crying in the wilderness:*
'Prepare the way for the Lord,
make a straight path for him.

FELIPE: "He was a man who lived in the desert, wasn't he?"

I told him that "desert" meant simply a remote place, without people, like in Nicaragua we say, "the mountains" or "the woods" (like this Solentiname place is called "the woods"). And through some manuscripts recently found in some caves it is now known that in those regions there were some communities, a kind of monastery, of a very religious sect called the Essenes. And surely John the Baptist lived with them (and Jesus' going into the desert meant that he was probably spending some time in these communities). But the Essenes lived in isolation and wanted no contact with the world, whereas John went to the "desert" not to be isolated but to send a message from there to the cities.

Every gulley shall be filled,
every hill and hillock shall be leveled.

OLIVIA: "It seems to me that happens only in a socialist society, where everybody lives equal. Capitalism is all gone and everybody lives like everybody else."

WILLIAM: "Yes, it means to level society. He

was preaching equality. The prophet Isaiah had used those images to say that a man was going to come preaching equality to prepare for the arrival of the Messiah, and that man was John. All the more reason why we should preach it, since the Messiah has come and we're trying to live Christianity. 'Every gulley shall be filled' means there'll be no misery and 'every hill and hillock shall be leveled' means that there won't be great wealth either."

And everyone will see
the salvation that God gives.' "

MARÍITA: "Everyone will see the liberation that God gives on the day that we get that equality. I believe those words of John are still real for us."

LAUREANO: "I believe we're preaching it here in the woods too, in the 'desert,' as John preached it."

When the people came to be baptized,
John said to them:
"O race of vipers!
Who warned you to flee
  from the terrible punishment
that is coming?
Behave in such a way that it will be seen
that you have changed your attitudes."

I said that here the Gospel used the Greek word *metanoia*, which means "change of mind." This word used to be translated as "conversion" or "repentance," but now these words have a purely religious meaning and this new translation, "change of attitude," is better.

FELIPE: "That's what's most fundamental, Ernesto. I think a person has to change his attitude so that it's noticed in his conduct. That's why he told them to behave in such a way that people would see that they had changed their attitude."

WILLIAM: "Because conversion can't be only inward. It does no good to be converted inside if we don't change society. They went there to ask for baptism so that their sins would be forgiven. John's message is change society so that it will be clear that you are converted. But all they wanted was the ritual."

FÉLIX: "They were coming to be baptized but they kept on being selfish. That's why he calls them a race of vipers. They were going there because all the people were going."

SABINO: "They were going there the way people now go to that famous medicine man, Nando. People come to him from all over Nicaragua, and he gives them water in a little bottle with some shells. . . . In the same way those people went to ask for water."

And don't go saying among yourselves:
"We are descendants of Abraham":
for I tell you that God can make
*   even these stones descendants of Abraham.*
The axe is now ready to cut the trees,
and every tree that does not bear good fruit
is cut down and burned in the fire.

OLIVIA: "He meant that they shouldn't feel like saints just because they were descendants of a saint like Abraham. They shouldn't believe that just because of that they were a saved people, because they were very far from justice."

ADÁN: "The same thing happens today with people who think they're within the Church because they go to Mass and receive communion, they take the child to be baptized. But they don't change their attitude. Those people are a race of vipers too."

PABLO: "Ninety-five percent of Nicaraguans say that they are Christians, but Christianity of that kind even stones could have it."

GLORIA: "And the tree that doesn't give good fruit is the person who doesn't do anything good for other people. The fruit is action, action to help other people, I mean."

Then the people asked him:
"What shall we do then?"
He answered them:
"The man that has two shirts
must give one to the man that has no shirt;
and the man that has food must share it
with the man that has no food."

LAUREANO: "If he said that to them, those guys must have been rich. Because if they'd been poor there was no reason to tell them to give to others."

FELIPE: "I think he was saying that to the

106

poor, too, creating that conscience in them, not to let their poor comrade starve to death. What I do believe is that this basic doctrine is the doctrine of socialism. John is telling us that this is the society that we have to create. That nobody ought to have one shirt more than his comrade.... We're going to be all equal. That's what we have to seek: socialism, because that way we'd all be living a just life, like God wants."

MANOLO: "If somebody who has two shirts has to give one away, there's even more reason for somebody who has several houses or estates or a million *pesos* ... "

WILLIAM: "I don't think this should be understood so literally—that if I have two shirts I have to give one away.... That's all right, but we're not going to stop there, just looking for somebody who doesn't have a shirt. What this means, it seems to me, is that we have to change the system where some people have lots of extra shirts and others don't have any. This is leveling the roads, as I said before."

I said that this applies mainly to the rich, as Laureano said, who do not only have many shirts but also houses, lands, factories, mines, railroads. But it can also be applied to the poor, as Felipe says, for example when one has to share his lunch with a friend ...

ALEJANDRO: "It's easy to share your meal with a friend. It's harder to share with people you don't know, with the rest of society ... "

FÉLIX: "I think this applies more to the *campesino* than to the rich, because the rich help one another, as long as they all have money. A rich person comes across another rich person and sees that he's naked and runs to give him a shirt and he doesn't have to be asked. Because it's among themselves, the one who has money helps out those who have money. But with us poor people it's different. If one of us has some little thing that God didn't give somebody else, he doesn't share it. And that's why that comparison of the two shirts is for us poor *campesinos*. And I think that us poor people are more selfish than the rich. We said that the reading of the Gospel is aimed more at the rich than at the poor, but it's not true. It's aimed almost more at us. The selfishness of the rich is that they don't look twice at the poor person because he doesn't have any money ... "

OLIVIA interrupts: "And how could you be any more selfish than that!"

FÉLIX: "Well, yes. But then if I'm poor I should also seek out my poor comrade. I meant that us poor are often more selfish than the rich. Among themselves they're good about money. Their selfishness is toward the poor."

WILLIAM: "But they murder each other. In business they all try to ruin the other guy."

FÉLIX: "The truth is that the nice thing would be if we were all equal. But John's word was not accepted in olden times and it's not accepted among us either."

JULIO MAIRENA: "What John says can apply to us, too, because we can all make a contribution to the struggle to take away from the guy that has a lot and so level ourselves off."

NATALIA: "There are times when we don't trust each other. If I don't have something—a dress, a meal—maybe I'll be embarrassed to tell anyone. But if you have trust then anybody can help you. Because if they're on close terms with me and they say to me, 'Look, Doña Natalia, . . . ' I tell them, 'Go ahead and take it. . . . ' But if they don't have that trust then there's no way I can know they need a little salt, a little sugar. But if they come to me and I have a little, I share it."

FÉLIX: "Lack of trust is because we don't have love. If I see a fellow full of love, I trust him enough to ask him a favor, to say to him, 'Look brother, I need this.' "

An elegant lady was with us who had come from the city, and she said: "Has it occurred to you that maybe some people have more than others because they've worked harder, and they've earned it through their own efforts? You know there are people that don't work and still want you to give them things."

JULIO MAIRENA: "We work all day long and we kill ourselves working with our machetes, and the rich are the ones who don't work."

TOMÁS: "You have to be careful, because if I have two shirts and I see that the other guy is a bum and won't work, well I'm not going to give him one of my shirts. But in this community we all work. Because if I don't want to work, because I'm drinking a lot, the other guy notices it and he doesn't give me anything and nobody else does either. Once in a while we've had a loafer, but they go away. It used to happen more. It's been getting better recently."

FÉLIX: "If somebody didn't work here he'd have starved to death by now. Even if you work hard you still have a lot of troubles. How about if you didn't work ... "

> *Some tax collectors also came to be*
> *baptized, and they asked John:*
> *"Master, what must we do?"*
> *And John said to them:*
> *"Don't collect more than the law says."*

TERE: "Could that law be just? Why does he tell them to obey the law and not to disobey it?"

I: "He's only telling them not to steal. It's not that he approves of the law. As long as the law existed ... "

LAUREANO: "These tax collectors weren't revolutionaries and that's why he said that. If they had been revolutionaries he would have told them to disobey the law. That's why they killed him, because he was against the authorities."

Some soldiers also asked him:
"And we, what must we do?"
And he answered them:
"Don't take anything from anyone,
either by threats or by accusing him
*   of what he has not done,*
and be content with your pay.

One said: "Good advice for the police. In those days there were already informers, right? Security agents. Secret police, like that Mario who used to come here and his name wasn't Mario."

Another: "It would be like if the captain from San Carlos came to this meeting that we're having here in the church and asked us what he has to do ... "

I said: "Even in the army, in the police, there might be some who want to be converted, to change their attitude, like these who came to John, and this is encouraging."

I indeed baptize you with water,
but one will come who will baptize you
with the Holy Spirit and with fire.

OCTAVIO: "The Holy Spirit is wisdom."

JULIO: "It's love for others."

GLORIA: "And the fire is love too."

EDUARDO: "Because it gives light and warmth."

TERE: "And also because it purifies."

And he now has his fan in his hand
to clean the wheat
and separate it from the chaff.
He will gather the wheat in his granary,
but he will burn the chaff
in a fire that never goes out."

FRANCISCO: "It seems to me that the chaff is the selfish person, empty of love for others, and wheat is the person who devotes himself to others. Wheat nourishes and that's why it's kept. Chaff is useless, no good for food, and it has to be thrown out."

ALEJANDRO: "A separation of the ones who are good for something from the ones who aren't. You don't keep what doesn't do any good. Humanity has to be divided into the good and the evil, the ones who love and the ones who don't."

TERE: "It's up to each one of us to be wheat or chaff. If somebody is useless it's because he's chosen to be like that."

And we finally saw that John the Baptist was jailed, because:

Besides, he reproved Herod the governor
for taking as his wife Herodias,
the wife of his brother Philip,
and also for the other bad things
    he had done.

MANOLO: "He reproved him not only for adultery but also for all his tyrannies and his crimes. That's what it means here by 'for the other bad things he had done.' He couldn't preach about a change of attitude without touching the person of Herod."

FELIPE: "And when the priest and bishops keep prudent silence in the face of the crimes that happen in this country, because they say that it's not proper for them to get involved in politics, they simply aren't following this example from the Gospel."

The elegant lady: "And don't you think that John would have been of more use to humanity if they hadn't put him in jail and killed him?"

TERE: "If he had kept silent he wouldn't have done any good. Martyrs may have been very useful during their lives, but they've been more useful to humanity as martyrs."

FELIPE: "He gave his message even better with his death than with his life."

13.

The Baptism of Jesus

(LUKE 3:21–23)

We were in the meeting hut, facing a very blue and very calm lake. We had rice and beans and fish for lunch. Tomás Peña had brought the fish, and Doña Tomasa had steamed them wrapped in leaves.

We read a short passage from Saint Luke (three verses) and we commented on it:

> *Before this, when Saint John was
>   baptizing all the people,
> Jesus was also baptized.*

I said, to start with, that "baptism" was a Greek word that meant "bath." It was a purification ritual that many peoples on earth had practiced. And I asked why it was that Jesus was baptized.

One of the women said: "To give us an example. He didn't need baptism but we did, and he did it so we would do it when we saw that even he did it."

Somebody else said: "And he could also have done it out of humility. He was with his people, with his group, and he wasn't going to say: 'I don't need this, you do it, I don't have any sin.' The others, the Pharisees, might say that, the ones who didn't follow John. Not Jesus, he goes along with the others."

And TOMÁS PEÑA: "He goes along with the rest of the people. Lots of people were going. He was around there, and went along with the crowd just like one more guy."

ALEJANDRO: "You could also say out of solidarity. So he wouldn't be separated from the group."

And another: "There are some people here who don't come to church because they think they don't need these things. And so they separate from us, from the community. Not Christ, he agrees to do this even though he didn't need to, so that he wouldn't be separated from the community."

And while he was praying,
the heavens opened
and the Holy Spirit descended like a dove
    in bodily form upon him,
and a voice from heaven was heard saying:
"You are my beloved son;
    I am well pleased with you."

"It wasn't that a dove descended, because it doesn't say that a dove descended but *'like* a dove.' A dove is a soft and loving little animal.

115

And the Holy Spirit is loving. It was the love of God that descended upon him."

"In this way the Father wanted to make it clear that he was pleased that Jesus had been baptized. He also wanted to show the meaning of baptism, which is to receive the Holy Spirit."

"God acknowledges him as his Son, and in the same way he acknowledges us too when we're baptized, when we change our attitude, not when we're baptized just out of habit as is done throughout the country."

"And this baptism becomes a true one when you become an adult, when you can choose a change of attitude."

I said: "It seems that this baptism of Jesus was the beginning of consciousness of his mission as Messiah, and of being possessed by the Spirit of God or the Spirit of liberation. In the Old Testament it had been prophesied that that spirit would descend upon the Messiah, and that's what Luke said came down upon Jesus in the form of a dove. Once when the Jewish leaders asked Jesus who had given him authority, he told them he wouldn't answer them if first they didn't tell him with whose authority John had baptised. In saying this he was telling them that he had received his authority or mission as Messiah in that baptism of John. At other times Jesus also spoke of his death as a baptism or 'bath' that he was going to have. He means that his true baptism would be that of his death, his blood bath, and this is

116

what he accepted when he accepted his calling as the Messiah."

Jesus was about thirty years old when he began his work.

I observed that traditionally it has been said that Jesus died at the age of thirty-three, but the Gospels don't give his exact age. They say only that when he began his public life he was about thirty, that is, a young man, and he could have been between twenty and thirty. He was what we would call a boy."

LAUREANO said, smiling: "I think he was about my age."

14.

The Temptations in the Wilderness

(LUKE 4:1–13)

We read how Jesus was taken to the wilderness by the Holy Spirit and there spent forty days fasting, and I said that this simply meant that Jesus probably had a period of retreat in one of those Essene communities, reflecting about his mission through prayer and fasting.

And afterward he felt hunger.
Then the devil said to him:
"If you really are the Son of God,
command this stone to turn into bread."
Jesus answered him:
"The Scripture says,
'Man does not live by bread alone,
but also by every word that God speaks.'"

FRANCISCO: "The devil wanted him to perform a senseless, useless miracle that wouldn't do anybody any good."

118

OLIVIA: "Or that would do good only for Jesus himself. Later he would perform the miracle of giving bread to a whole crowd, but that was different. Here we were dealing with a selfish miracle."

GUSTAVO: "And I see that more than anything else the temptation consisted in reducing his messianism to a purely material level—a developmentalist messianism. Of course, bread is important, but we can't stop there. Revolution doesn't mean just giving food and clothing and comforts to people. It goes beyond that. And this was a temptation that Jesus had as the Messiah, and he rejected it."

TOMÁS: "Bread is food. Animals live only on food. People live on another food too: the bread of love, or the words of these meetings that we're having here, I mean the Eucharist."

MANUEL: "Christ says that food isn't enough for human life. Just like animals can't live without food, people can't be truly human without the word of God. Without it a person isn't human like other people. He's an animal, a wolf..."

ELVIS: "To teach us that, that we need the word of God for life, he had gone into the wilderness to fast."

And MARCELINO: "The word of God gives us bread too. Because in a community some might have bread and others might not. And if

119

there's love we share it and we all eat. If there isn't any love, even though there's a lot of food people will be hungry because a few people will hoard the food."

ÓSCAR: "The word that God speaks is love, because that's the message God has given us and Christ brought to earth."

We went on to the second temptation. The devil takes Jesus to a very high mountain and shows him all the kingdoms of the earth. This is something that he must have seen in his imagination, I said.

> *And the devil said to him:*
> *"I will give you all this power*
> *and the greatness of these kingdoms.*
> *For I have received all this*
> *and I give it to anybody I choose.*
> *If you will kneel down and worship me,*
> *it will all be yours."*

LAUREANO: "He's like a politician, that devil. Because that's what political campaigns are like. A man comes into a town and makes all kinds of promises so people will vote for him. And people do vote for him and afterwards he doesn't give them shit."

Another says: "The devil wanted Jesus to adore him so he could be God."

And another: "He was offering him an imperialist messianism."

"Then imperialism would be all right if it was the imperialism of Jesus?" asked JULIO.

FELIPE: "No, because if Jesus had fallen into temptation his imperialism would have been just like the others."

TOMÁS: "Just like theirs, because they're under the power of the devil."

TOÑO: "There's one thing here: The devil is making him a false proposal. He tells Jesus that he's going to give him all the power and the riches of the world, and Jesus, by refusing, is stating that the true master is himself, that is, all of humanity. And he doesn't have to adore the devil to get him to give Jesus what is rightly his. And that's our situation, too."

I said: "Why do you suppose the devil says that he has received all this?"

WILLIAM: "He grabbed it all. It's a dictatorship. He has the power, but a power that's not legitimate. It's stolen. Imperialism and capitalism and all oppression belong to him. It's up to us to take from the devil what he has grabbed for himself—the riches of the earth. This temptation of Jesus is also a picture of what's happening now: Those in power offer things to the people so that they'll serve them ... "

FRANCISCO: "And from what we see in this passage, all governments are of the devil. Christ couldn't set up a government like that. He came to make a Revolution against all these powers. And there will have to come a day when there isn't any government. Then the Revolution will be a complete success."

And FELIPE said: "The devil declares that he is the owner of the kingdoms of the earth. This must be because when he was condemned the devil fell into the depths of the earth, into the abyss. And so he believes he's the owner of the earth. It's not true, but he thinks he owns it. And he wants it all for himself, like a dictator, like an exploiter. And everybody who wants to take over the earth is like the devil. But they don't own the earth, because the only way to own the earth, it seems to me, is in little lots—and little lots all equal."

ALEJANDRO: "When the devil showed Christ in the spirit all the countries he must have been showing him the cities and the governments. Not the lakes, the mountains, the volcanoes, because they aren't evil, they don't belong to the devil."

MARCELINO: "Power. All power is evil and it comes from the devil."

TOMÁS: "The devil offers him all this so that he'll adore him, I mean so that he'll become haughty and selfish, so that he'll go over to his side."

I said: "It's true, the devil is the master of pride, of haughtiness, of the power of people over people. This is his nature, and this is what he gives to his people. That's what he offers to Jesus and Jesus rejects it."

Someone else comments: "Riches don't belong to the devil. It's the selfishness of the rich—that belongs to him."

Afterwards the devil
   took him to the city of Jerusalem
and he took him up
   to the highest point of the temple
and he said to him:
"If you are truly the Son of God,
cast yourself down from here;
because in the Scripture it says:
'God will order his angels to take
   care of you . . . ' "

TOMÁS: "The devil told him to fly off the roof of the temple because he didn't have faith that he was the Son of God. He wanted to know if he was or wasn't. That's why he said that to him."

ÓSCAR MAIRENA: "The fact is that the devil was testing him out: If you really are, throw yourself down."

Another said: "He's suspicious."

And another: "He's confident. What's happening is that he wants to control the Son of God, to have more power than him, and so he gives him orders to see if he obeys. And so we see the great power that he has in the world . . . "

And the journalist PEDRO RAFAEL GUTIÉRREZ, who once had a top position on a government newspaper and who now lives with us: "I see a picture here too: The devil took Jesus up, just as he seizes many of us and lifts us into certain positions. It says: 'He seized him and he took him up.' So to some he gives riches, he gives power, he gives greatness. And once these people are powerful then comes the temptation to screw the weak, to oppress them. And he said: 'No, don't tempt me!' As I see it, there is a temptation of the devil, which is to raise people up, to lift us to the heights and then let us fall."

JULIO MAIRENA: "And it's a useless miracle that the devil proposes: to throw himself down and have angels save him. What for? That wouldn't do anyone any good. That was a show-off temptation."

WILLIAM: "As I see it, this is a messianic temptation too. Throwing himself down from the temple without anything happening to him would be spectacular. Imagine if it was on a feast day and all the people were gathered there. And he presented himself as the Messiah dazzling the masses with his miracle. And Jesus refused to be this kind of a Messiah. Later he would go to Jerusalem during the feast, but in a different way. He rejected the temptation: He told the devil to go to hell. But the Gospel says the devil 'went away for some time. . . . ' Afterwards the bastard came back."

"Yes," I said, "in fact these three temptations are a single temptation: that Jesus present himself as the commanding and triumphant Messiah that the Jews were waiting for. And this would be a real temptation for him. And he rejected it, knowing that liberation for him had to come through suffering and death. When the Jews asked him for a great spectacular sign, he told them that the only sign he would give them was that of Jonah (his death and resurrection). And this temptation not to accept his passion and death, to be another kind of Messiah, he would have it again in Gethsemane."

FELIPE PEÑA: "I see that the devil tempts him by saying 'because the Scriptures say.' It's just like a lot of Catholics and Protestants use the Bible to defend their interests. They say: 'The Scriptures say such and such a thing. . .' And it's all to exploit us."

And another: "It's like when they say to the poor: 'You've got to respect the property of the rich because it comes to them from God.'"

And still another: "And there's another temptation too: not doing anything, thinking all you have to do is pray, like a lot of Catholics believe; or read the Bible and be very religious, like a lot of Protestants believe."

Jesus returned to Galilee
filled with the Holy Spirit,
and there was talk about him
in all the region around.

ALEJANDRO: "He went to the wilderness guided by the Holy Spirit, and there he was filled more with the Holy Spirit—with this retreat that he had with God, and with the temptations that he overcame. He came back with more love, that's what 'filled with the Holy Spirit' means. He was convinced that he had to be humble and poor to be the liberator of the

125

poor. The devil had tried to make him dizzy with greatness ... "

TOMÁS: "He received more of the Holy Spirit so that he could suffer and bear it, I mean because of what he was going to suffer at the time of his death."

And I said it was interesting to see that when he was filled with the Holy Spirit, he set out on no other journey, began no other project. Instead he returned to his home, to the humble people where he had been brought up.

15.

Jesus in Nazareth

(LUKE 4:16–30)

We were in the little church, and we read the Gospel passage where Jesus goes to the temple in Nazareth and reads a prophecy of Isaiah:

> *The Spirit of the Lord is upon me*
> *because he has chosen me*
> *to give the good news to the poor;*
> *he has sent me to heal the afflicted*
> *   in heart,*
> *to announce freedom to the prisoners*
> *and give sight to the blind;*
> *to set free the oppressed,*
> *to announce the year of grace of the Lord.*

Somebody began by saying that here we see how Jesus wasn't against the Scriptures but against the Pharisees who falsified them in the temples and used them to defend their interests, even though the message of these Scriptures was liberation.

I said that *evangelio* [Gospel] is a Greek word that means "good news," and the translation that we read here, "to give the good news to the poor," is better than the one that has been traditionally given, "to evangelize the poor." The expression "good news" in antiquity had the sense of joyful announcement, of a message of joy or victory. "Good news," an *evangelio*, was announced when a prince was born, when a battle was won, when the emperor was going to visit a city. When the messenger or evangelist arrived with some "good news" there was great rejoicing. Emperors often sent false "good news" so that great feasts would be held in their honor at the people's expense. In reality the "good news" was always a false joy, and for the people it meant the announcement of a new oppression. When Herod came to power the cities of Galilee would receive one of these "good news" or *evangelios*. In the time of Christ the word was a political term associated above all with the cult of the emperor, who was considered a god and a savior. Just by using this word, Christ was indicating that his announcement was the announcement of a new kingdom.

And others comment:

"And his good news is for the poor because this new kingdom is the triumph of the poor and the humble."

"And this is truly good news, not like the others, which were false."

"And it's a joyful announcement for the whole people, one that deserves to be celebrated."

"And it's news that we can believe in or not."

One of the women says: "What he read in the

book of that prophet is prophecy of liberation. And it's a teaching that a lot of Christians haven't learned yet, because we can be in a church singing day and night tra-la-la-la, and it doesn't matter to us that there are so many prisoners and that we're surrounded by injustice, with so many afflicted hearts, so many people without education who are like blind people, so much unfairness in the country, so many women whose eyes are filled with tears every day. And if they take somebody else prisoner, what do we lose? 'Maybe he did something,' they say, and that's the end of the story."

FELIPE adds: "Prisoners, in every sense. Yes, because it's not just the ones who are in jail. It can also be a servant, a prisoner of a rich person, serving him. Also, the ones who are prisoners in their mentality, without any freedom to think. Their minds have been so conditioned that the only thing they know how to do is to serve."

And one who has come from the opposite coast: "And to put up with whatever they do to them. Because that's how it is; if we're serving some rich person we're putting up with whatever they do to us. They don't even let you go out, because if you go out to take a rest you lose your job. 'We're going to have to let you go,' they tell you. And so you don't lose your job, there you are, putting up with things until Sunday."

And another: "And if we talk about this they say it's communism. That's what the radio

129

says hour after hour: It's communism. What they mean is that they like keeping us in slavery."

I explained that the "year of grace" that Isaiah speaks of and that was also called the "holy year" was a year of general emancipation of people and goods, which Yahweh had ordered to take place in Israel every seven years. Bought slaves should then be freed, all debts should be abolished, and lands that had been sold should be returned to their original owners. The aim of this measure was to guarantee equality and freedom, to prevent the monopolizing of the lands. The law later decreed that the year of grace should be every fifty years (the jubilee), and it was really a law that was not carried out. The prophecy of Isaiah was that the Messiah was going to announce a Lord's year of grace that would be definitive.

WILLIAM: "And the holy or jubilee year now means that people go to Rome to pray in the churches and receive a papal blessing. But the holy year should be agrarian reform and the socialization of all means of production."

Another: "A holy year is what's been done in Cuba . . ."

Then Jesus rolled up the scroll,
gave it to the attendant of the synagogue,
and sat down.
As all eyes were fixed on him,
he began to speak and he said:

*"Today this Scripture
has been fulfilled in your presence."*

PEDRO RAFAEL GUTIÉRREZ: "Of course. Just by announcing liberation he was already fulfilling this prophecy. And just by saying 'today this prophecy is fulfilled' he was announcing liberation."

WILLIAM: "The Scripture said that he was going to say those things. He just had to read the Scriptures for them to be fulfilled. The good news was proclaimed to the poor."

PEDRO RAFAEL: "And so he makes it clear, with deeds more than with words, that he is the Messiah, the announced liberation. This was his first political manifesto."

OLIVIA: "And from his own lips we heard that those words are for him. And this is how they were fulfilled. Not only those words that he read there but all the other words of Scripture. That's why they're so interesting for us."

NATALIA: "And now it's up to us to follow those words. I'm sure not everyone believed."

And TERESITA: "It's like an invitation that he gave, to liberty."

WILLIAM: "He's saying that he's the one. It's a message of pure liberation: the poor, the afflicted, the blind, the imprisoned . . . "

LAUREANO: "The truth is that all those people—blind, imprisoned, afflicted—they are the poor."

PEDRO RAFAEL: "And you have to see, as a contrast, the negative part too. He didn't come to give any news to the rich but to talk to the poor. He didn't come to give health to those who are happy but to those who have problems, to the afflicted. He didn't come to be the ally of those who put people in jail but to free the prisoners. And he didn't come to blindfold people's eyes but to make them see. And he didn't come to oppress but to put an end to oppression and to proclaim total liberation. Let nobody falsify these words, as it often happens. And he said it in church!"

COSME: "We see clearly, as Marcelino said the other day, that the world is very different from the way Christ wants it."

And I: "An example of how his words have been betrayed is that instead of saying that he came to give joyful news to the poor, it's been translated that he came to 'evangelize the poor.' "

> And they were amazed at his beautiful
>   words and they said:
> "Is this not the son of Joseph?"

FELIPE laughed and said: "It's as if they were seeing somebody who's the son of Octavio or of somebody around here, a carpenter, a laborer . . . "

"What he says is true," added old TOMÁS, who can't read. And he continued: "They can say the same thing about these poor people: 'Isn't that so-and-so?' "

Somebody else cited the case of a neighbor who doesn't want to come to our meetings because he says what can he learn hearing comments on the Gospels from *campesinos* as ignorant as he is and he said: "If only the people who talked were educated! But all that you're going to hear is a Marcelino, an Alejandro, a Laureano . . . "

And I said: "That's exactly what they said about Jesus. The good news is for the poor, and the only ones who can understand it and comment on it are the poor people, not the great theologians. And it's the poor who are called to announce the news, as Jesus announced it. You would have to make our friend see that liberation can come only from the poor. And another time Jesus gave thanks to the Father because he had hidden this from the learned and he had revealed it only to the poor and the humble."

He said to them,
"Surely you will quote to me this proverb:
'Physician, heal yourself.' "

REBECA: "Because he was poor. Let him liberate himself before he liberates others. They don't understand that he has to be poor to liberate the poor, and he can't do it if he's rich."

JULIO: "They could say the same to us in Solentiname . . . "

And he added:
"In truth I say to you

that no prophet is welcomed
in his own country."

TOMÁS: "We're sure that's how it is . . . "

PEDRO: "It proves what he told them because right there they took him out and tried to kill him."

MARCELINO: "Jesus is present again in the temple announcing the good news, and he does it through the mouth of this poor community. And the Scripture that's just been read has been fulfilled right here."

16.

The Man Who Had an Evil Spirit

(LUKE 4:31–37)

Then Jesus went to Capernaum,
a town in Galilee,
and there he began to teach people
*   on the day of rest.*
They were amazed at how he taught them,
for he spoke with words of authority.

"We see," I said, "that Jesus has had to go away from his own town because nobody is a prophet in his own country. He goes to another town, Capernaum, and there he enters another temple."

And FÉLIX said: "They were surprised to see that he was a poor man like them, and that he went around maybe in dirty clothes, like them, and his teachings were not the kind that would come from a man with dirty clothes. Last Sunday we heard them say in the other temple: 'He is the son of a carpenter, a workman; the son of a laborer; we know his father and he's a workman.' And here too they're surprised that

135

he speaks with authority. A laborer talking with authority."

And the patriarchal TOMÁS PEÑA with his steady voice: "It seems that Jesus was beginning to sprinkle his Gospel around. And it seems that he makes them see from the start that he has more authority and more power. A man like all the others but with an authority that the others don't have. He was a poor man speaking with authority. It's not only the rich that can speak with authority. Here's a poor man who speaks with more authority than the rich and he speaks against the rich. A poor man with more authority than all of them. The people must have been surprised. They wondered at the way he taught them."

In the temple was a man
who had a demon or an evil spirit,
who cried:
"Leave us alone;
why do you meddle with us,
Jesus of Nazareth?
Do you come to destroy us?
I know you, and I know
*   that you are God's Saint."*

ÓSCAR: "It must be that he wanted to have more authority than Jesus, and that's why he got so mad at him. Since Jesus was putting him aside and getting rid of him, so that he wouldn't be a nuisance, he got angry. 'Don't meddle here,' he said, 'go away.'"

ADANCITO: "I'd like to ask one thing. What kind of people nowadays say: 'Let Jesus go away"? And who think that the Church is giving them false propaganda? Who don't want the message of the Gospels to be preached so the poor won't understand that Jesus came to bring good news to the poor, to the laborers, to the oppressed, to the exploited?"

And FELIPE PEÑA, the son of Tomás: "Why, the opponents, the exploiters. If God speaks through the poor now, it's probably the exploiters who will say: We don't want these words of God."

I said that certainly those who commit injustices have to say: "Don't let Jesus come to meddle here." And this Gospel that we preach here in Solentiname must get them very mad. I also said that it was interesting that the demon should call Jesus "God's Saint," which is the same as saying "Messiah." He knew very well who he was, and that's why he wanted him to go away.

And JULIO, Óscar's brother: "Like somebody who reads the Bible a lot and knows God's message very well, but out of selfishness doesn't accept the message. Because it's harmful to him. The demon realizes that Jesus is the Messiah and that he was coming to liberate people, and that's why he didn't want him to meddle with them. He doesn't attack Jesus because he's evil. He attacks him for being God's Saint, and he didn't want to have anything to do with that."

Another said: "He was sincere."

137

And one of the ladies added: "There are rich people who know that the Gospel speaks of sharing the wealth. And they don't want to listen to the Gospel. They're sincere in that too."

Jesus answered the evil spirit saying:
"Be silent, and leave that man!"

TERESITA: "That's what you can say to a person who's defending oppression. That's the way to shut him up."

LAUREANO: "And wouldn't it be, too, that he shut him up because this evil spirit was denouncing him? Because he's calling him God's Saint, which means Messiah, Liberator, and he shouted it so all the people would know it and would screw him. It's like if someone came up to me here in church and shouted: 'You're a communist!' And that's another reason why Jesus shouted to him: 'Be silent!' "

JOSÉ: "It said before that Jesus taught with a lot of authority. And here he spoke with even more authority and he silenced him once and for all. There he showed his authority by ordering the demon to leave the man: 'Be silent and leave this man!' "

Then the evil spirit threw the man
  to the ground in front of them,
and came out of him
  without doing him any harm.
They were frightened and they said:
"What words are these?

This man gives orders to the
evil spirits with authority and power,
and they leave!"

ÓSCAR: "They were frightened because they were on the side of the evil one. And when they heard these words they saw that he had more power than they or rather, than the devil had. And because of this they were puzzled and thoughtful. They said: 'He can do more than this one.' "

EDUARDO: "They saw that he was leaving people free ... "

MARÍA: "That's why they said, 'What words are these?' Because they had already heard his words, his teachings, which were words of liberation. And now they see them fulfilled."

TOMÁS: "The demon also walks around here among us and we're tempted by him at every step. He walks around here, in some places more than in others ... "

ALEJANDRO: "In Solentiname less than in others, in Managua more than here."

FÉLIX: "There the evil one does all kinds of evil."

And there was talk of Jesus
in all the places of the region.

One said: "And so the authorities were already on their guard, from the beginning of Jesus' ministry, because of what was shouted by that devil who was a spy."

And another: "Every spy is somebody with an evil spirit, but the spirit can leave him, like what happened to that man who was freed. The same thing could happen to that spy Mario that we had, whose name wasn't even Mario. This system we have put that spirit in him, but he can be free too some day."

And PEDRO said: "And don't you think it has a special meaning that the Gospel tells us that the man with the evil spirit was in a church?"

17.

The Miraculous Catch

(LUKE 5:1–11)

We had gone to celebrate the Eucharist on Deer Island, and we were gathered in the open air near the hut of a *campesino*, with the lake in front of us, deep blue, and our boats very close to us tied to the shore. A boy from Deer Island had read:

Jesus saw two empty boats on the lake,
near the shore,
for the fishermen had left them
and they were washing their nets.

And NATALIA said: "When he saw the boats and the nets on the shore he decided to go fishing, too. And he got into a boat and sat on the gunwale and began to tell them his parables like a fisherman throwing out his net. When he saw the people crowded on the coast, he felt like he was a fisher of people. And then he got the idea of inviting the owners of the boats to become fishers of people, too."

DON JOSÉ CHAVARRÍA, who lives on Deer Island: "The news had spread all over that he was the Messiah and the poor people came looking for him to liberate them from all their troubles and afflictions and he had pity on them and got into the boat to give them his message of liberation from there. And when he saw that there were a lot of them and that there were a lot more in the whole messed up world, then he said to the ones who were fishing there: 'Change your jobs, help me to liberate these people.'"

> *When he finished speaking,*
> *he said to Simon:*
> *"Take the boat to the deep part*
> *and cast your nets to fish."*
> *Simon answered him:*
> *"Master, we have been working all night*
> *without catching anything;*
> *but since you command it*
> *I'm going to cast the net."*
> *When they did so they caught so much fish*
> *that the net began to break.*

Old TOMÁS PEÑA, who is a great fisherman: "Maybe all this happened because they'd been having hard luck. They'd worked all night without catching a single fish. There was no point in throwing out any more nets. But since he said so ... Simon said: 'I'm going to throw it!' Just out of faith in him. It wasn't because of anything else. He knew they were having bad luck."

And somebody added: "It was because of that faith of his that they made that catch."

And still another said: "He called him **Master** because he listened to his teachings. He wasn't just worried about washing the nets."

FELIPE: "I think he saw him like somebody who was leading them, and he was teaching them something very real."

JULIO: "Even though he was one of them. He was a working man. Simon wasn't following him yet. He was just the owner of the boat. But he hears these teachings that Jesus tells the people from the boat, and from then on he calls him Master. And when Jesus tells him to cast the dragnet, he obeys him. He tells him: 'But since you command it, I'm going to cast it.' Do you suppose this has anything to do with our lives?"

"Of course it can," said DON JOSÉ. "It makes us see that faith is everything. Because he already understood, even though he was an ignorant man. He was already coming to know who Jesus was, and he had a great faith."

"A man who has no faith has nothing," exclaimed NATALIA.

And I said that we find a practical lesson for ourselves: that with faith we can perform miracles.

TOMÁS PEÑA: "As I see it Jesus was sorry for those people and wanted to help them. And he sees that a miracle would be a good thing, but he can't give them riches because you don't get saved with riches. You get corrupted instead. And then he orders Peter, or Simon

Peter, to perform a humble miracle: to catch fish. A miracle not of riches but of humbleness. Nobody was going to get rich from it, but they were going to believe in his word, in his humble teaching. So here among us anybody who wants to perform miracles shouldn't go thinking that making riches is performing a miracle. Because for miracles you have to be humble."

I asked whether there wasn't some other teaching of Jesus in that humble miracle of a net with fishes.

And one of the boys from Fernando Island said: "Maybe I see it, Ernesto. Because it seems to me that the business about the net and the fish is to picture for us another miracle he was going to perform later. Because this miracle of the fish, maybe we were seeing it before only as the fish in the net, but now we see something else. Because the net could have been his teaching, and the fish could have been us, going into the net."

CHAEL: "Do you remember that song, how does it go?"

Several (singing): "You have to let yourself be caught . . . "

NATALIA: "Caught by Christ! Caught!"

FELIPE PEÑA: "Yes, by Christ! Not by anybody else. You have to know who you're going to let catch you. Because that's what I see here in the net and the fish. And the first one caught was Peter."

When he saw this,
Simon Peter knelt down before Jesus
and said to him:
"Go apart from me, Lord,
for I am a sinful man."

ÓSCAR: "Maybe he has the experience, then, of being a sinner. Of course, he was one, just like any one of us is a sinner, but he hadn't felt it before. And now, when he saw himself involved in the miracle, well, he felt bad, I don't know, all beaten down, like."

And one of the Altamiranos of Deer Island, who catch sawfish, said: "Maybe the fish is a kind of lack of faith, right? Faith in yourself, in other people, in everyone, right? Because this isolates you. If you don't have faith in anything, well, you're isolated. Lack of faith is a sin, then. Peter lacked faith, and that's why the Master told him to cast the net, right?"

JULIO MAIRENA: "I believe this way, Ernesto. Look: The world is always full of complexes. The poor have a complex about smart people and about the rich (who are educated). Peter felt inferior, felt that he couldn't stay in God's presence, since he didn't know that Jesus was coming for the sinners and the poor. And he didn't take into account that Jesus, even though he was smart, was also a poor man himself. He thought they couldn't be in the same place together."

145

I said that perhaps this complex that Julio was talking about was the same one that the Gospels described as a fear. And we read the following verses:

Because Simon was amazed,
and also all those who were with him,
by the catch that they had made.
Also Jacob and John, the sons of Zebediah,
who were companions of Simon,
    were amazed.

MARCELINO: "I think you'll always find this fear in the poor. If one fellow has cash, the poor think that he'll be able to order them around and that they can't resist. And somebody with a lot of education makes us feel useless too. We're always afraid that somebody who is more educated is going to reject us."

But Jesus said to Simon:
"Do not be afraid;
from now on you're going to be
    a fisher of men."

DON JULIO GUEVARA, who was also a famous fisherman: "He wanted to tell him in a word that he was going to be equal to him, right? Jesus was a fisher of men."

And one of the young people said: "He looked for country people and fishermen to do his work, not aristocrats. And it's because the workers are the ones who really transform the world and are called to be the masters of the world. Even though a lot of them don't know it; but Jesus, he knew it."

146

One of the girls: "Of course he wasn't going to look for bums, exploiters, parasites of society. He looked for workingmen, people with a job, like these fishers of fish that he made into fishers of men."

And one of the ladies: "So they in turn could look for other humble people, that nobody paid any attention to before. People who didn't count for anything. Just like Jesus told Peter to cast the net where he thought there was nothing, and up came a terrific catch."

OLIVIA: "Think of this: All us people gathered here used to be scattered, with our own self-ishness and individualism, slipping away from each other, as slippery as fishes... We're the miraculous catch."

Then, when they brought the boats ashore,
they left everything
and went away with Jesus.

Young JULIO: "Well, they went away with him out of the faith they already had in him. And what they were taking away was a marvelous thing, confidence in this miracle worker who performed the miracle of the big catch for them and at the same time the feeling that somebody so miraculous had confidence in them ... "

NATALIA: "Then they abandoned their belongings. Yes, they left the boats right there and the nets."

RODOLFO: "Probably a rotten boat like the one that belongs to the Cooperative."

NATALIA: "They were poor, but they had their few things. The way poor people do. And they left their things right there and followed Jesus."

DOÑA ÁNGELA: "They let themselves be caught by him."

Another of the boys said: "That was the miraculous catch, and not the haddock and shad and mojarras and all the other different fish they caught with the net. And they caught us and that's why we're gathered here, as Doña Olivia says."

MARCELINO: "Because they left their belongings right there, the word of God came to these islands. Perhaps later we can carry the word to the other side of the lake too. To Papaturro, or maybe San Carlos, San Miguelito . . . "

DON JULIO: "Before we used to be only fishers of fish from the lake here, but now we can be fishers of men too, if we get rid of our belongings."

And FELIPE said: "That's the thing, Ernesto. I think that since we are or are going to be fishermen, we have to be very careful not to want to fish for our own personal interests. In Christian religions there are a lot of people who are just trying to take advantage of others. And the catch of Jesus Christ is for the good of humanity. It's the catch of love."

ALEJANDRO: "Maybe a lot of times we feel like somebody who's worked all night without catching anything, and he's all worn out, and he doesn't want to fish any more. And we feel that other people in other parts of Nicaragua and in other countries are the same way; they haven't caught anything. But let's not be discouraged, because this is a miraculous catch. And when we least expect it the terrific catch will be brought up."

When we finished, a fresh breeze was blowing from the south and the lake was beginning to ripple.

18.

The Wedding at Cana

(JOHN 2:1–12)

We commented on the Gospel in the meeting hut after we had a lunch of rice and beans with some breadfruit that Octavio brought from Stork Island.

We read how Jesus went with his mother and his disciples to a wedding in a small town.

> *The wine was gone,*
> *and Jesus' mother said to him:*
> *"They have no more wine."*
> *But Jesus answered her:*
> *"Woman, why do you tell that to me?*
> *My hour has not yet come."*
> *But she said to those who were serving:*
> *"Do whatever he tells you."*

I said that Jesus' words—"Why do you tell that to me?"—according to the latest biblical studies, are very strong words. In other parts of the Bible they always appear in lawsuits or when someone is being injured by someone

150

else, and it's something like our expression "Stop bugging me."

I waited to see what their comments would be and, after a long silence, OLIVIA spoke: "His hour, which hadn't come, was the hour of his death. He shouldn't be performing miracles yet, presenting himself as the Messiah who was coming to do good and to liberate the people, because then the powerful would kill him. That's why he says to her: 'Woman, stop bugging me, my hour hasn't yet come.' "

We all saw that the explanation was very clear. There was another long pause, and then MARCELINO spoke: "Following up on what Olivia said, I see that Mary's attitude is a good example. Jesus may have been afraid. It's very natural for somebody to be afraid of death. Later he was afraid in the garden when his hour came. Or maybe it was just prudence. It's all the same. But anyway Mary here doesn't seem to be afraid or to pay any attention to prudence, but she urges him to perform the miracle. He didn't want to get into being a Messiah yet, and she pushes him into it. It seems like she's saying: 'It doesn't matter if they give us a hard time.' And she calls the servants."

ALEJANDRO: "That's the way that every revolutionary mother ought to be with her revolutionary son. Instead of trying to talk him out of it, telling him 'don't get involved,' she urges him to fulfill his mission. She pushes him."

WILLIAM: "This reminds me of the conversations that Father Camilo's mother said she used to have with her son, after dinner, when he got mixed up in politics. He would say to her, 'Mama, when they kill me ... ' And she would say, 'Son, when they kill you ... ' Here Jesus is simply telling her that they're going to screw him. It was a fact that the two of them had already calmly accepted."

CARLOS ALBERTO: "It was all because of a nice couple who had invited them and who were going to be in a mess and the only thing to do was to perform the miracle. By doing this he was already pushing himself into his public life, I mean, into struggle, and now he was going to begin to be persecuted. I see that right after this, in the following passage, Saint John already has Jesus driving the money changers out of the temple, and also talking about his death. So it's clear that this miracle speeded things up."

And MARÍA VICTORIA, the wife of Carlos Alberto: "It's clear that she already knew he was in agreement, because she doesn't answer when he tells her that she's getting him involved. She just calls the ones who are serving so that he can give them wine."

MANUEL: "And isn't it interesting that Jesus gets himself involved for a party? His hour will come sooner because he gave wine at a party. It wasn't for something more serious."

ÁNGEL: "It must be to show us that liquor is

good, and that people can be happy at a party. We see that Christ didn't think like the Protestants of the Church of the Nazarene, who say that it's a sin to drink or smoke or dance or sing..."

And JESÚS CHAVARRÍA (CHUCHÚ), a young man who was studying in Masaya and who had come here for a week: "But it was also because afterwards he was going to change the wine into his blood, in the Eucharist."

There were six stone jars there,
of the kind that Jews use in their
    purification ceremonies.
Each jar could hold
    about eighty to a hundred quarts of water.
Jesus said to the servants:
"Fill these jars with water."

PABLO HURTADO: "By this he shows that he had no respect for these purification ceremonies. The conversion of the purification water into wine is also a symbol of the conversion of the legalistic law of the Jews into a law of love. If all the water that they had for purifying themselves turned into wine on them, now how were they going to perform their ceremonies? I'm sure some of them must have asked him: 'Master, and now how do I purify myself?' And he must have answered them: 'The orders are to have a drink.'"

DON JULIO: "I see one thing: Those jugs held a lot of water. That means that they held a lot of purification. They were very extreme. And he went to the other extreme by giving them a lot of liquor."

PABLO: "Six hundred quarts. They really got plastered."

I said: "There were people who didn't drink wine and who fasted a lot, the Essenes . . . the disciples of John the Baptist . . . very strict people like those brothers of ours who go to the Nazarene Temple on Carolina Island. And they were probably scandalized to see Jesus perform such a profane miracle."

> *The man in charge of the party*
> *tasted the water that had turned to wine,*
> *without knowing where it was from;*
> *only the servants knew,*
> *for they had drawn the water.*

ÓSCAR: "It seems to me that the wine means joy, a party. To be happy. Enjoyment. Also love. He wanted to make us see that he was bringing enjoyment, happiness, a party."

OLIVIA: "Joy. And also unity. Wine unites. He was coming to bring about unity among people. But liquor can separate too, and lead to quarrels, stabbings . . . "

ÁNGEL: "Also, when rich people drink liquor in selfish parties, it doesn't create any unity. There's no brotherhood there—at least, for the poor people who are being excluded . . . "

I said that in the Old Testament the messianic era had often been described as an epoch of great abundance of wine. The prophet Amos had said that when the Messiah came there would be great harvests of wheat and grapes, and that the hills would distill wine. Isaiah says that God was going to prepare a banquet for all the peoples, with very good meat and very good wines. And he had also prophesied about the Messiah, saying that "he would not be sad." By this miracle Christ is making it clear that he is the promised Messiah.

MARCELINO: "We see then that he was coming to bring unity and brotherhood among people. That's the wine he brought. If there's no brotherhood among people there's no joy. Like a party where people are divided, where they don't all share alike, it's a party without joy. A person's birthday or saint's day is not a happy party if there's division . . . "

"Or if they stab each other," said ANDREA, Óscar's wife.

MARCELINO went on: "So a society with quarrels, with social classes, can't have a true banquet, a true party."

WILLIAM: "The party will be the kingdom of God, that new society. And that's why Christ, when he said goodbye to his disciples at the Last Supper, he told them that he wouldn't drink wine any more until he drank it with them in that kingdom."

CARLOS ALBERTO: "He also spoke of his doctrine as a wine. The new wine that breaks the old wineskins . . . "

FELIPE: "I think that Jesus liked to drink. He made his first declaration as Messiah with wine. He also made his Eucharist with wine. They accused him because he drank with sinners. He said that in the kingdom he was going to get drunk with us, or that he was going to drink wine with us (the same thing). What *is* clear is that he didn't want to drink alone, or with a few people the way the rich do while most of humanity suffers, but with everybody, even with the poorest little person, and that's why he'll drink with us even in the kingdom of heaven. There there'll be wine in abundance, and not just wine, because there are people that drink other things: beer, rum, *chicha*, *guaro*, *cuzuza*. And there'll be plenty of liquor there, because he'll be with us."

PABLO: "You remember when he said that his disciples didn't fast like Saint John the Baptist's disciples because they were celebrating because he was the bridegroom, but when they killed him then they really would fast? He means that now we can't have celebrations or parties like the rich have because Christ is still being crucified in the poor. Not because parties are evil or fasting is good, like the disciples of John the Baptist believed, but because of solidarity with the poor."

JOSÉ ALANIZ, Olguita's husband: "I think we should ask for wine for everybody, like Christ taught us to ask for bread in the Our Father. Bread and wine are equally important. Bread is the food and wine is the joy, and that's why he made one miracle with bread and another with wine. Because there are so many poor people, who don't have any parties, drunken brawls maybe, but not joy. The joy of the kingdom will come when everybody loves each other and everybody is friends."

TERESITA, William's wife: "But it wasn't at any old party that he performed the miracle. It was at a wedding party."

OLGUITA: "The wedding meant that he was coming to bring love."

I said that it had often been prophesied also that the messianic era would be like a wedding with God. Isaiah had said to Israel: "As a boy marries a girl, so he who formed you will marry you, and as the husband enjoys his wife, so you will be the delight of your God." And I said too that the Song of Songs is a book that speaks of that wedding. There the wife asks him to kiss her and says that his caresses are better than wine. He tells her that her eyes are like doves and that her breasts are like two fawns grazing among the lilies. She says that the time of the songs has come, that the rain has ended, and that the vines are fragrant. He tells her that her love is better than wine, that under her tongue are milk and honey, that her belly is like a little hill of wheat surrounded by lilies, that in her he has drunk his wine and his milk. And she says that she exists for her lover and her lover exists for her. Jesus wanted to make it clear that with his arrival, this wedding was now here. John the Baptist, when he called him Messiah, had called him the bridegroom. And Jesus himself said that his disciples didn't fast because he was the bridegroom. And in several parables he spoke of the kingdom of heaven as a marriage, or as a wedding feast, and of himself as bridegroom.

FELIPE: "There will be no lonely people, no frustrated ones then, will there? This love is going to be for everyone, for every single one. No one will be excluded from that wedding. That will be true social justice."

JOSÉ ALANIZ said: "That's right. You don't just need bread and wine and all the harvests. You also need love. You have to satisfy that need of love."

I said: "That's right. No one will be left without those kisses, without that wine of the Song of Songs."

OLIVIA: "Everybody, men, women, old people, children, even nursing babies, we all form a single body: humanity, the bride loved by God."

LAUREANO: "Or we're struggling to form it. This struggle is the Revolution."

ALEJANDRO: "Now I see more clearly why we all have to love each other. Now I see it very clearly: humanity, men, women, children, everybody, is a wonderful thing now that God is in love with it. And if it's so wonderful for him, it must be wonderful for us too. And so it's very important to make it be perfect, be holy, and this is the Revolution."

CARLOS ALBERTO: "God is Love. Humanity is going to get married to Love."

And so the one in charge
called the bridegroom and said to him:
"Everybody serves first the best wine,
and when the guests have drunk quite a bit,
then the ordinary wine is served.
But you left the best wine for the last."

ÁNGEL MAYORGA: "It's obvious. At the beginning of a party you serve *Flor de Caña* Rum or *Victoria* Beer. Afterwards, when everybody's loaded, you serve *cuzuza*." (Everyone laughs.)

OLIVIA: "The joys of the world are best at first and afterwards they change into disappointments. With the joy that God gives it's just the opposite."

MARCELINO: "It seems to me that the joy of brotherhood, the perfect society that God is preparing for humanity, that's the great party. But the best wine of that party will be the last one: eternal life."

19.

Jesus Cures a Leper

(LUKE 5:12–16)

We read how a leper approached Jesus and knelt down before him and said:

Lord, if you want to,
you can clean me of my illness.

One of the girls said: "It seems to me that he said that, sure that Jesus would want to. He knew that Jesus could do anything if he wanted to, and that's why he said 'if you want to.' Begging him as a favor, but sure that he was going to cure him."

And ÓSCAR: "I think he said 'if you want to' because he didn't feel worthy, he felt inferior, and that's why he said 'if you want to.' He didn't feel he could demand anything of God. He was a leper, a fellow people looked down on. He told Jesus, 'If you want to, all right, and if you don't, don't.' And Jesus' answer was that he did want to. It was a humble thing the man did. He wasn't forcing Jesus in any way. That's the way us Christians should act, not wanting to force God. He felt very humiliated because of his sickness, he was a leper. He didn't feel like he was a son of God."

And another of the young men: "He probably said that also because he was already realizing he was in the presence of a person greater than everyone, and he felt like a sinner when he faced this person. Maybe that's why. He's recognizing a divine power facing him, who could cure him just by wanting to."

A lady: "He must have been thinking of all the cases where God didn't cure, because he didn't want to. Because a lot of times there are sick people who are sick because God wishes it. And Jesus wasn't curing everybody either. He cured some."

PEDRO RAFAEL said: "And as soon as he asked Jesus for this favor, he was already converted to him. Because he knew that Jesus was the only one who could cure what couldn't be cured. And his plea was an act of faith."

WILLIAM: "He recognizes Jesus as the Liberator from all evils too, even from sickness and death. Lepers at that time were like dead people. They couldn't go into the city or have any contact with people."

And OLIVIA: "And he recognizes that when Jesus wants to, he cures, and when he doesn't, he doesn't. The leper recognizes that if Jesus

161

wants to cure his illness he can cure it, and that if he doesn't cure him it's because he didn't want to."

And NATALIA: "We don't know, do we, why sometimes he doesn't want to cure our sickness, or why he sends us one."

Then Jesus touched him with his hand
  saying:
"I do want to.
You are clean."
And as soon as he said this
the leprosy left the sick man.

OSCAR: "The leper isn't forcing him. He goes to Jesus to see what he wants, to cure him or not to cure him. And Jesus wants to cure him, and he does."

FÉLIX MAYORGA: "We should also notice that Jesus cures people who ask for a cure. If he hadn't approached Jesus he wouldn't have cured him. Because notice he never said: 'I don't want to.' He always wanted to, but he was waiting . . . "

I said: "With a request like that he wasn't going to say: 'I don't want to.' "

OLIVIA: "There are so many Christians that want to force God or the saints with their prayers. They even make promises, which is like trying to buy God."

I said: "The leper's words are an example of how we should pray, telling God to do with us what he wishes. If he wishes health, if he wishes sickness, if he wishes death. But only things that don't depend on us should be considered as the will of God. In those days leprosy was incurable. Now there are leper hospitals where it can be cured. The illnesses of the children in Solentiname have cures. And the evil we can overcome we shouldn't consider as the will of God."

Then Jesus commanded him
  not to tell this to anyone.
He told him:
"Just go in and present yourself to the
  priest,
and for your purification
give the offering that Moses ordered,
so that all may know
that you are cleaned of your illness."

TOMÁS: "It seems to me he told him not to tell anyone because he understood that he would maybe say something else that wasn't true. But the sick man went to tell it sooner because he saw that it was an interesting thing, and so he said: 'I better tell it.' "

DONALD: "That's very strange: He tells him not to tell but he sends him to the temple to be purified so that the people will know that now he's healthy."

ELVIS: "It seems to me that Jesus didn't want publicity. Because he knew there was a class of people opposed to him, and so it was dangerous for them to begin to give him publicity. I don't know how the others feel."

OLIVIA: "But he wasn't afraid, because he knew that in the long run they were going to kill him. That his hour was going to come. Earlier he said: 'My hour has not yet come.' What *is* true is that he didn't like publicity. If *we* don't like people to give us publicity, much less Jesus who was divine. People weren't going to keep quiet, but it wasn't because he told them to spread the news. The sick man himself, once he was cured, just by showing people he was healthy would make it known that there had already been a miracle. And I think that always happens, that publicity is unnecessary because I think that truth always makes itself known."

I said that the two interpretations seemed to me very true: He didn't want publicity because he wanted to be able to do his work quietly without the interference of the upper classes. And also he didn't want personal publicity. He was a leader who didn't want power or glory, but only to carry out his work.

DON JULIO CHAVARRÍA: "I see that he asks him not to tell anyone who cured him, but to go to the temple to show that he's healthy. He didn't have any reason to say in the temple how he'd been cured."

WILLIAM: "That was so they wouldn't reject him even more. Leprosy, syphilis, and other skin diseases were considered impurities. A leper was like someone excommunicated, he couldn't approach people. This leper had already broken one law, as the Gospel makes clear, when it says that he 'approached' Jesus. Jesus tells him not to tell, just to go and ask for a health certificate, so that he can again become a member of the human community."

ALEJANDRO: "That was a very human act of Jesus. If somebody has the power to relieve the hunger of a person who's dying of hunger, just as an example, then he ought to relieve his hunger. But the revolutionary has another mission: It's not to relieve the hunger of a few individuals or to cure a few people but *all* people, right? So Jesus doesn't want to concentrate on little details like this or to have a lot of publicity about it. What he came on earth to do was a bigger thing ... "

LAUREANO interrupted him: "Just like Che had to take care of sick people as a doctor in the Sierra Maestra ... "

ALEJANDRO continued: "He did those cures because he had to. How could he say no to the man? But this wasn't his mission and that's why he told the man to keep quiet. And he didn't want to get a reputation either, and be confused with a medicine man ... "

MANUEL: "So what if they *had* taken him for a Nando, the medicine man from Matagalpa. He attracts so many people they even arrive in buses to get cured by him! But since leprosy also was considered impure, when he cured him he wanted to make clear what his mission was: to cure humanity of all its ugly sores, because the humanity that he found was like a man covered all over with leprosy."

FELIPE: "It's clear to me. He wasn't coming

just to do those petty little things. Like us, right? A revolutionary group can give a mouthful of food, some clothes to a guy that doesn't have any. But this isn't their goal. It's to liberate the whole country. That's how it was for Christ. Along the way he had to do those little jobs. A very good lesson for us."

I: "He was coming to cure the real sickness, which is selfishness. When it's liberated from selfishness, humanity is liberated from all other sicknesses, even leprosy. In a society without selfishness there are good doctors, medical attention for everybody, hospitals, a cure for leprosy. And yet the leper hospital in Managua is so horrible that, as I just read in the paper, some foreign technicians have recommended that they close it and send the lepers back to their homes."

WILLIAM: "And I notice that when Jesus sends the man to the temple to present the offering required by the law of Moses, he doesn't do it to comply with a religious precept. And he himself makes it clear to him what the reason is: 'So that everyone will know that you are now clean.' "

TOMÁS: "Since he was sick they didn't let him go around with people. Now that he's cured he tells him to go so they'll know he's healthy and so he can go around with people, it seems to me. So that they wouldn't be disgusted by him anymore."

But the fame of Jesus increased
   more and more,
and many people came together
to listen to him and to be cured
   of their diseases.

"You see? The government must have been getting nervous," somebody commented.

But Jesus would go away
to solitary places to pray.

We had as a visitor a Salvadorean exile, a professor, who left El Salvador during the military occupation of the university, and he said: "The Pharisees used to use the temple, the house of God, to do business. That's why Christ of course wouldn't go to the temple to pray but went away to a solitary place. Now, too, many people can pray better in their houses than in temples that are used badly."

FELIPE: "People who made money off religion as they do now."

TOMÁS: "Yes, if people were selling things there, why should he pray there? It was better for him to go into the woods. In the woods you can pray very well."

WILLIAM: "I wanted to add something but it's about what we were talking about a while ago. When he cured the leper, it's very significant that he touched him. When he did that he put an end to the taboo that lepers were untouchable. And he could have cured him without touching him, but he did touch him. He teaches us by this to make contact with others, especially with anyone who suffers. And he also teaches us to cure that way. There are good doctors, loving doctors, like Fernando Silva, who put their hand on you where it hurts. And they use this to cure you, too, not just medicines. There are doctors, on the other hand, the kind that people complain about: 'He didn't even touch me.' Because maybe they gave a prescription, but there was no love, no contact of the doctor with the sick person."

I said: "In the communities of the first Christians this is what was called 'the laying of hands on the sick,' something they had learned from Jesus. Afterwards it came to be just a ritual, but in those times it was a curing power like what we have seen in Fernando Silva, a power that Jesus has transmitted to his disciples."

FELIPE: "It's very important that he had touched that sick man. Like touching a consumptive who disgusts everyone. If we touch him we'll get what he has, we have to stay away from him!"

PEDRO: "Coming back to the prayers: Christ was a man who was very fond of prayer. When he speaks of the temple he doesn't say that it's a place of worship. He calls it a 'house of prayer.' He went away to pray at Gethsemane when he saw he was going to die. He taught us to have contact with his Father, just like he had contact himself. And he prayed to his Father when he was dying. Christ was a man of prayer."

I said: "He told the Samaritan woman that later there would be no temple, that people were going to be able to have contact with God without useless formalities or ritual ('in spirit and in truth'). The true temple is the community, the presence of God is there, but he teaches us another lesson: God is also in solitude."

20.

The Beatitudes

(MATTHEW 5:1–12)

We read that Jesus went up to a hill, and said to his disciples gathered around him:

Blessed are the poor in spirit,
because theirs is the kingdom of heaven.

I said that in the Bible the poor are often called *anawim*, which in Hebrew means "the poor of Yahweh." They are so called because they are the poor of the liberation of Yahweh, those that God is going to liberate by means of the Messiah. It's like what we now understand as the "oppressed," but in the Bible those poor people are also considered to be good people, honorable, kindly and holy, while their opposites are the oppressors, the rich, the proud, the impious. This word *anawim* was probably the one that Jesus used. In Greek there was no word like that, and when the Gospel of Matthew was translated into Greek that word was translated as "poor in spirit," whereas Luke in his Beatitudes says simply "the poor." This phrase of Matthew, "poor in spirit," has created confusion, and many have believed that it deals with spiritual poverty. And I said that I met a priest who said that the "poor in spirit" were the good rich people.

OLIVIA: "The poor in spirit or the poor in God are the poor, but provided they have the spirit of the oppressed and not of the oppressors, provided they don't have the mentality of the rich."

TOMÁS PEÑA: "Because us poor people can also have pride, like the rich."

ÁNGEL: "Us poor people can also be exploiters. As for the kingdom of heaven, I say what I've already said other times, that Matthew calls the kingdom of God the kingdom of heaven because of the Jewish custom of not mentioning the name of God out of respect, but that doesn't mean that the kingdom is in 'heaven.' In the other Gospels it is called the kingdom of God. Jesus surely must have used the same words Matthew used, because as a good Jew Jesus would follow the custom of not mentioning the name of God. Because of this expression Christians have for centuries wrongly believed that he's speaking only about a kingdom in the beyond."

And MARÍITA said: "It's here on earth, but it's also in heaven after death."

Another said: "Yes, because there are so many poor people who die without having any happiness, and why are they called happy then?"

171

And another: "Like little old Don Chico who just died all alone. When they found him the ants were eating him."

And LAUREANO, who always talks about the Revolution: "But you can't forget that the kingdom is here too. Because they're thinking about heaven, poor people often don't fight."

His cousin ÓSCAR: "Well, if they don't fight for their brothers and sisters and their children they don't get to the other kingdom after they die."

And ÓSCAR'S MOTHER: "It seems to me that the kingdom is love. Love in this life. And heaven is for those who love here, because God is love."

FELIPE: "Jesus said that because he knows the poor are able to put love into practice better, right?—which is the kingdom that God brings us. Then he blesses the poor because they're the ones who are going to make this new society of love."

"And it's because the rich couldn't practice love, then," said JULIO.

I asked why not. And he answered: "Because of their great selfishness, they can't say that they can love. But the poor can, because as oppressed people they do not exploit and they are less selfish."

I said that was true, that the rich in some way always made money at the cost of the poor, making other people work for them, and using the money from that work to make more money at the cost of more work by others. Then, as long as it's that way, as Felipe says, they can't love their fellow human beings, unless they divide up their riches and stop exploiting.

ÓSCAR: "Ernesto, I also think that the poor person can practice love more sincerely, without being afraid, and fight for it, without being afraid of the word of God. But the rich person can't because it doesn't suit him. Even though he may know what's good, he doesn't practice it, because he is always ready to screw people, to exploit them. And that's why I think a rich person can never be sincere, while the poor person can. And God sees the poor person's sincerity and promises him the kingdom of God."

MARCELINO: "The way I see it is that the man who owns a business whether he needs money or doesn't need it, he's always doing business. The poor person says: 'I have a piece of *tortilla* and somebody else doesn't have any, so I'll give him some of my piece.' There is a difference between the spirit of the man who owns a business and the man who doesn't own one. I was talking with a man and I was saying: 'What would you do for a man who was in great need and you were selling a boat that cost a thousand *pesos*, would you let him have it for five hundred?' And he said to me: 'Why should I? Business is business.' And he's a rich man."

"Well, that's just why he's a rich man," somebody answered.

And ALEJANDRO: "What we see here is that there are two things. One is the kingdom of God, which is the kingdom of love, of equality, where we must all be like brothers and sisters; and the other thing is the system we have, which isn't brand new, it's centuries old, the system of rich and poor, where business is business. And so we see that they're very different things. Then we have to change society so that the kingdom of God can exist. And we're sure that the kingdom will have to be established with the poor, right?"

PANCHO: "With everybody that shares the love, because if there are rich people that share the love, they too can enter the kingdom."

MARÍITA: "But a rich person that shares love has to share his goods too. That's how he shows that he shares love. Because if he says he has love and doesn't share his goods, how are we going to believe him?"

REBECA: "But it's all the same. Some of us, even though we're poor, we don't inherit the kingdom of God either. If we're poor and don't have love. And there are rich people who have the kingdom of God, if they have love."

ÁNGEL: "That's why it seems to me that we have to interpret carefully. If we just stick to the fact that we're poor and God has said that the kingdom of God is for the poor, then we'd end up saying that, well, since we're poor we already have the kingdom of God and we can do anything! And the rich are going to be condemned because they're rich. So we have to interpret carefully what God says. Let's not think that just because we're poor we already have the kingdom of God."

ÓSCAR: "I think we have to be clear about this. You either love God or you love money. You decide to make money? Well, go love your money, that's your god. Somebody else loves God? He shares his money and is poor. Then he really can live love."

PANCHO: "But there are rich people who share ..."

JULIO: "But maybe just a little. And it's to quiet their consciences. Or they give away their money but they give it, maybe, for great temples, for huge churches with good-looking saints, and they don't give a damn for their neighbor, shit on their neighbor. And I don't think that's sharing love, in my thinking."

I said: "Then we're quite clear about what the kingdom of God is, and why Jesus blesses the poor, telling them that that kingdom will be theirs. The other Beatitudes seem to be only other ways of saying the same thing. In all of them the same poor people are spoken of by other names, and what they promise is the same thing."

Blessed are those who are sad in heart,
for God will give them consolation.

Blessed are the humble in heart,
   for they shall inherit the earth
   that God has promised them.
Blessed are those who hunger and thirst
   for justice, because they will be fed.
Blessed are those who have compassion
   for others, for God will have compassion
   for them.
Blessed are those with pure hearts,
   for they shall see God.
Blessed are those who bring about peace,
   for they will be called the children of God.
Blessed are those who suffer persecution
   for the sake of justice,
   because theirs is the kingdom of heaven.

First we commented on the sad in heart, who will have consolation.

TOMÁS PEÑA: "I look at, how shall I say it, the relief that Christ gave to the poor when he came, because they felt so alone, and the rich were rich, and the poor were almost an abandoned class. And then when Christ came he gave them that consolation. Us poor people, the poorer we are and the more we suffer, then the happier we must be because we have been chosen for the kingdom. Well, that's what I think. But others think different. And then we don't follow what the Book says here, and maybe we get things confused."

And FELIPE, his son: "Well, it may be something for the poor to be proud of to know that we have been chosen for the kingdom. But we also have to remember that Jesus doesn't want people to go on being oppressed. He came to liberate humanity, so that the world won't be divided into rich and poor, and he doesn't want everyone to be poor. We can be happy about the news that the kingdom is coming, but we can't be satisfied until it comes."

REBECA: "And he blesses those of humble heart. It seems to me that these are the poor in heart or the humbled. Maybe they were even humbler before (that's my idea anyway) and yet for God they were the most worthy. People shouldn't feel sad, then, even though they are poor, poor in spirit or humbled, because God will bring them into the Promised Land, which is the kingdom. But those of proud heart will not enter."

ESPERANZA, a little girl, asks: "Can there be a humble rich man?"

MARÍA, her sister: "Not unless he shares his wealth."

NATALIA: "Because the first Christians shared everything: land, money, houses, boats."

I said: "And it's clear that the first Christians, as we're told, before they had been given the name of Christians had given themselves the name of *anawim*, because they considered themselves the poor of the Beatitudes. And there were no rich among them because they shared everything, but neither were there any who were in need."

MARCELINO: "He blesses those who hunger

and thirst for justice. Hunger and injustice amount to the same thing. Anyone who hungers for food also hungers for justice. They are the ones who are going to make social change, not the satisfied ones. And then they'll be filled with bread and social justice."

Young JULIO: "When there's a revolution in a country the poor aren't hungry anymore, and they are already building, it seems to me, as it says here, the kingdom of heaven among them. As long as there is hunger, injustice, sickness, well it seems to me that the kingdom of heaven is very far off."

ALEJANDRO: "He blesses those who have compassion. I believe that it's those who have compassion for others that become revolutionaries. There are many who are poor, or who are middle-class city people, employees who earn their little salaries but they're not rich, yet they still have the ambition of the rich. And if some time some of them get rich, they might be very cruel. Rebeca pointed out that the poor of Jesus Christ are those who practice love. The poor who are bourgeois, who are opposed to revolutionary changes, they do not have compassion in their hearts, and they are not the poor of the Gospel."

LAUREANO: "A perfect communism is what the Gospel wants."

PANCHO, who is very conservative, said angrily: "Does that mean that Jesus was a communist?"

JULIO said: "The communists have preached what the Gospel preached, that people should be equal and that they all should live as brothers and sisters. Laureano is speaking of the communism of Jesus Christ."

And PANCHO, still angry: "The fact is that not even Laureano himself can explain to me what communism is. I'm sure he can't."

I said to Pancho: "Your idea of communism comes from the official newspaper or radio stations, that communism's a bunch of murderers and bandits. But the communists try to achieve a perfect society where each one contributes his labor and receives according to his needs. Laureano finds that in the Gospels they were already teaching that. You can refuse to accept communist ideology but you do have to accept what you have here in the Gospels. And you might be satisfied with this communism of the Gospels."

PANCHO: "Excuse me, but do you mean that if we are guided by the word of God we are communists?"

I: "In that sense, yes, because we seek the same perfect society. And also because we are against exploitation, against capitalism."

REBECA: "If we come together as God wishes, yes. Communism is an equal society. The word 'communist' means community. And so if we all come together as God wishes, we are all communists, all equal."

WILLIAM: "That's what the first Christians practiced, who had everything in common."

PANCHO: " I believe that that communism is a failure."

TOMÁS: "Well, communism, the kind you hear about, is one thing. But this communism, that we should love each other ... "

PANCHO: "Enough of that!"

REBECA: "It is community. Communism is community."

TOMÁS: "This communism says: Love your neighbor as you love yourself."

PANCHO: "But every communist speaks against all the others. That means they don't love each other."

ELVIS: "No, man. None of them talk that way, man. They do tell us about their programs. And they're fine."

FELIPE: "The Gospel blesses the poor who have clean hearts. The truth is that they're not all like that, because many have the mentality of the rich. Especially since it's the rich who educate us. On the radio, in the ads, they are forcing their mentality into us; it's completely the rich man's."

WILLIAM: "What Felipe says is quite true. The poor person naturally looks forward to getting out of his misery. But advertising creates false needs in the poor person, making him yearn for what he doesn't need. To build the kingdom of love (and that is to see God) you must be stripped of those ambitions, you must have a clean heart."

MANUEL ALVARADO: "It seems to me that ambition is what makes for disputes and that's why he blesses that kind of poor people, because they don't try to strip anybody of anything. If you're going to take somebody else's land away from him, you need a weapon. That's why there are so many armaments in the country. If I have a worker and I make him work for a wage that doesn't give him enough to eat, I'm not looking for peace, I'm looking for war."

ÓSCAR: "If I'm trying to have one person not exploit the other, I am one who is looking for peace. He says that people who look for peace will be the children of God, because they look for unity, that we should all be brothers and sisters. It's clear that the kingdom of God belongs only to the children of God."

His brother JULIO: "These peacemakers want to put an end to the class divisions that divide humanity, and that's why they fight, but it's not so that they can oppress others but so that nobody will oppress anybody."

ALEJANDRO: "And he says that they are going to be persecuted because they seek justice, and for that also he blesses them. Because it's clear that people who look for this kingdom have to be persecuted. The other day I heard somebody say that there were a lot of people afraid to come to church because there was talk in church against the system. They were afraid they would be informed on, or that something would happen to them, it seems. And they themselves, the next time they see you, they look at you in a certain way. It's not proper to talk about the poor and these things."

I said: "I've just had a visit from a young fellow from the north, from Estelí, from a poor town. He is a *campesino* like yourselves, and he was saying that there, to get together for their Masses first they have to ask permission from the police, and the police captain said that those gatherings were dangerous. The captain is right, for they gather there to talk about the Gospels. Those Christians of the earliest Jewish community, who had taken the name *anawim* before they were called Christians, were so called not only because they were poor but also because they were persecuted. Because 'poor of Yahweh' (or 'poor in spirit' in these Beatitudes) is the same as saying persecuted."

TOÑO: "That didn't use to happen here because the Masses were in Latin. The priest read these things but he read them in Latin, and he didn't explain them to the people. So the Gospels didn't bother the rich or the military."

And we went on then to the two final verses:

> *Blessed are you, when people insult you*
> *and mistreat you*

and say all kinds of false things against
  you because of me.
Rejoice and be glad, because you will
  receive a reward in heaven;
for like you the prophets that lived
  before you were persecuted.

OLIVIA: "Before he talked of people persecuted for looking for justice and now he says 'because of me.' He wants to point out that it's the same thing. Everyone who is persecuted in the cause of justice is persecuted in his cause. Here he is talking of insults and bad treatment, he's not talking of death. It must be because death is only in extraordinary cases (even though it can also happen). The most frequent thing is the insults and bad treatment. We're seeing it right here. They call us communists. To them that means bandits, evil people. Afterwards maybe they'll treat us badly."

JULIO: "We have to speak of injustice, even though they say we're into political maneuvering or communism, and that people shouldn't go to our church now. People who talk like this are getting away from the true Gospel, and they're getting isolated. It seems to me that this is where we ought to feel proud, because we are not into exploitation or evil. We're just spreading the true Gospel."

WILLIAM: "And Jesus compares us with the prophets. The prophets in the Bible were not so much people who predicted the future as people who denounced the present. They were protesting against the celebrations in the palaces, the cheating on the weights and the coins, the things that they bought very cheap from the labor of the poor, the swindles of widows and orphans, the abuses committed by the mafias of priests, the murders, the royal policy that they called prostitution, the dependence on foreign imperialisms. And it's true they also predicted something for the future—the liberation of the oppressed. Christ says that our fate has to be like the fate of those prophets."

And another one (a member of the Youth Club) added: "What Christ says, that they will say 'all kinds of false things against you,' we have already seen it—when that spy was here who informed the Office of Security that a Peruvian was here inciting us to rebellion. And he described these Masses as meetings of conspirators, and he even gave the names of the owners of the boats that came and the number of people that came on each boat, and he said, as if it was a serious thing, that these Masses were attended by a lot of young people. Those prophets were very great men and I think it's a great honor to be compared to them, and so we ought to feel happy. And also happy for the reward we'll have in heaven, which is the same kingdom of heaven that's been promised before."

MARCELINO: "This is what the 'good news to the poor' means. The news that theirs is the kingdom of heaven."

21.

"Woe unto You Rich . . . !"

(LUKE 6:24–26)

The previous Sunday we had seen the Beatitudes for the poor, according to Saint Matthew, and now we were going to see the curses for the rich that Saint Luke put after his Beatitudes.

> *But woe unto you rich,*
>   *because you have already had your joy!*
> *Woe unto you who now are full,*
>   *because you are going to be hungry!*
> *Woe unto you who now laugh,*
>   *because you are going to weep in sadness!*

I said that it was curious that the reason these rich people were going to be punished was just because they were rich, because they had already had their joy, not precisely for having been evil rich people.

TOMÁS PEÑA said: "Maybe they *are* evil. They are people who are treating the poor people bad. Or maybe they don't even want you to mention God, just because they've got money. And you don't have any, and you're always thinking of God or seeing what they do to get their things. And they, maybe, instead of giving, maybe they take away. That's what they've been doing for some time, and we're abandoned. It seems like it can be that way."

ALEJANDRO: "It's logical that the Gospel should put in this counterpart, because if it only said Beatitudes for the poor you might think that there's maybe another kind of Beatitudes for the rich, or for certain rich people, or that Christ is with the poor but he's also with the rich. But Saint Luke makes it clear that it's not that way. For Christ humanity is divided into two well-defined classes, and he's in favor of one and against the other."

LAUREANO: "This is very revolutionary. He says that all those who are well-off are going to be screwed. This turns the tables completely."

OLIVIA: "I think that what Jesus is condemning in them is lack of feeling. Because you have to have a hard heart to be happy while others are suffering, to be full of food while others are hungry—maybe the very people that work for them."

MARCELINO: "Not only lack of feeling. It wouldn't be so serious if they enjoyed wealth that came down to them from heaven, but their wealth is produced by the labor of others. A man has a cotton field of two thousand acres, but *he* doesn't farm two thousand acres. Other people farm the two thousand acres for him. And if he gives a party, it's with the product of that work. Instead of giving, they take away, as Don Tomás says."

WILLIAM: "The prophets when they prophesied the future announced the salvation of the oppressed and the ruin of the oppressors. The two things correspond. They couldn't talk about salvation for everybody. And Christ preaches along the same line."

FELIPE: "It seems to me that here Jesus has put himself on the side of the poor. But the Gospels can also be the liberation of the rich. Because this change, whether they like it or not, will make them fulfill the Gospels, even though by force. But we Christians must not wait for God to do this. We have to work for it. And I believe we have an obligation to work for the liberation of the rich. Some people say, 'What's it to us. Leave the rich the way they are, because they've got all they want!' But I believe that Christianity should preach to them. Christ did. It's clear that he also had rich people before him, because he's talking to them: 'Woe unto you the rich.' "

ALEJANDRO: "It's not as though when the Revolution comes they're going to be hungry or miserable. Nobody'll be miserable then. But when they lose their property they're going to feel as though they're miserable, as has happened to many who have left Cuba. And they're going to feel hunger, but it's only the hunger of their ambition."

OLIVIA: "But this refers to the other life too.

Those people that Christ was talking to didn't have to leave Cuba. Nothing happened to them. They always had everything. And so if Christ's threats are not fulfilled in the other life, then they were in vain."

I said: "I believe that this social change is in this life and in the other."

And we went on to the last verse:

Woe unto you when all speak well of you,
for that's what their ancestors used to
do with the false prophets!

I said that it had always interested me that in Christ's eyes it was bad that *all* should speak well. He did not consider the case in which opinions were divided and bad people spoke well but the good ones spoke badly, or the opposite.

CHAEL: "Could it be that the good are so few, just a handful?"

TOMÁS PEÑA: "Or they are many, but poor. And many of us, like me, can't read, much less write. So nobody pays any attention to our opinions. Jesus said: 'When all speak well...' or 'when all speak badly....' He's talking about all those who speak. Those on the radio, for example."

LAUREANO: "The priests who are on the side of capitalism, for example. On the radio you hear people speaking well of them. And the protesters. You hear people speaking badly of them. The stations are against the rebel priests."

I said: "It is true. Some people in Solentiname have been very surprised, and have been shocked, when the radio has spoken badly of me. But there's no reason to be surprised. The Gospel says woe unto us if all speak well. It says that that is what happened with the false prophets. In the Bible, alongside the true prophets many times the false prophets appear. They were on the payroll of the courts and they were the ones who defended the policies of the kings, soothed the consciences of the rich, led the people astray. They were opposed to any announcement of a change. Their prophecy was that nothing was going to happen, that the status quo would be maintained. Or as Isaiah says, their message was: 'Tomorrow will be just like today.' It's interesting what Jesus says about these false prophets, that *all* speak well of them. It is obvious. Everybody, even those who wrote history, has been on the side of the system of exploitation. The only book that was against it was the Bible."

TOÑO: "Those false prophets began preaching only good things to the people they were leading. They're like the ones who write now in the official newspaper."

TOMÁS PEÑA: "As we say here, they were on the inside ... "

And I: "They were on the inside, as Tomás says, that is, on the side of power and the status quo. And Christ says woe unto us if we choose to be on the inside."

22.

The Salt of the Earth and the Light of the World

(MATTHEW 5:13–14)

We were gathered in the church, at Sunday Mass. We were commenting now on a very brief passage:

You are the salt of the earth.
But if the salt loses its taste,
how can it be salted again?
It is now no good for anything
except to be thrown out
and trampled by the people.

ADÁN: "It seems to me it's because every meal should have salt. A meal without salt has no taste. We must give taste to the world."

JULIO: "By liberating it. Because a world filled with injustice is tasteless. Mainly for the poor, life like that has no taste."

MARCELINO: "You only need a little salt, because it's strong. You add just a tiny bit. There are only a few of us, but we can give taste to the world."

One of the Altamiranos, who are fishermen from Deer Island: "Salt is also for preserving foods. A sawfish, a shad, we salt it and it keeps."

And DOÑA ADELA, a little old woman with a weak voice: "We are the salt of the world because we have been placed in it so the world won't rot."

ÓSCAR, in a loud voice: "But also we're a salt that sometimes doesn't salt for shit. That kind of Christianity we've got to get rid of because it does more harm than good."

OLIVIA: "It seems to me that the salt has got lost when instead of preserving justice on earth, Christians have let injustice multiply more, as has happened now in capitalist society. We Christians wanted to prevent that, but we haven't. Instead, Christians have sided with injustice, with capitalism. We have sided with selfishness. We have been a useless salt."

FELIPE: "Christianity that stopped being Christian, that's the salt that doesn't salt any more."

LAUREANO: "Christianity that stopped being revolutionary, that lost its taste."

I said that once when I said Mass in Cuba, the Gospel of that Sunday was this one about salt, and I told them in my sermon that the same thing had happened to their Christianity. It was salt that no longer salted and that's why it had been thrown out and trampled, because God wasn't interested in keeping a Church like that.

ELVIS: "It seems to me that the very same thing is happening right now here. Christians don't have that Christian taste. They're simple-minded, insipid. Only the ones who are struggling for a just society are the ones who have that taste of salt."

ÓSCAR: "Ernesto, I'm going to ask you a question. Why is salt also considered to be a curse among us? When somebody has bad luck they say to him, 'You're salted!' "

I told Óscar that I didn't know. Perhaps it was because in ancient times when a conquering army wanted to lay waste a region it threw salt into the fields, the way the Americans now use defoliants. Jesus was probably not talking of salt in the sense of anything harmful but of something good. But salt and all the other things of the earth can be used for good or evil, as a blessing or a curse. I later said that in the Gospel according to Saint Mark there is another sentence of Jesus about salt: "Have salt within you and live in peace one with the other." I asked if anybody wanted to comment on it.

PANCHO: "I had always wracked my brains with that one, trying to understand it and not being able to. I was just going to ask you about it and now it's come up. I'm glad because I want to hear the explanation, what it means."

OLIVIA: "It's like saying, 'Love each other.' "

MARCELINO: "I think that 'salt' is the Gospel word given to us so that we'll practice it and pass it on to others, practicing love, so that everybody will have it. Because salt is a thing that you never deny to anybody. When somebody is very stingy they say that 'he wouldn't give you salt for a sour prune.' That's why Jesus says 'have salt,' which means to have love shared out among everybody, and so we'll have everything shared out, we'll all be equal and we'll live united and in peace."

PANCHO: "Doesn't it probably mean that in spite of sin and injustice, which have always got to exist, and in spite of the salt or bad luck that is our lot, we must live in peace with one another, rich and poor?"

LAUREANO answers quickly: "How can we live in peace when some people are hurting others?"

SILVIO was at this Mass, the son of Don Fidelmo, the leading merchant in San Carlos, and SILVIO said: "Only with love can there be peace."

OLIVIA: "It's all the same, 'have love,' 'have salt.' "

MANUEL: "Yes, because anyone who doesn't have salt is sick."

You are the light of the world.
A city that is on a hilltop cannot be hidden.

FÉLIX MAYORGA: "Maybe the light is the good people, who practice love. Everyone that has a good spirit and loves others, he is the light of the world. They set the example and the people will follow them, as someone follows a person that carries a lamp to light up the darkness. Or let's suppose we're lost in the dark, and there's a light. The guy that's lost looks for the light."

MARCELINO: "A lit up city that's on top of a hill can be seen from far away, as we can see the lights of San Miguelito from very far when we're rowing at night on the lake. A city is a great union of people, and as there are a lot of houses together we see a lot of light. And that's the way our community will be. It will be seen lighted from far away, if it is united by love, even though we don't have the city houses, just huts like the ones we have now, scattered here and there. But this union will shine and it's going to be seen from San Miguelito, from Papaturro, from San Carlos. And we may even get to be a city, too, because then we won't be in scattered huts the way we are now, and we'll have electric light, and when somebody goes by in a boat he'll see those lights of our union. But the thing that will shine most, and that's what Christ is talking about, is love."

23.

The Offenses

(MATTHEW 5:21–26)

*You have heard that your ancestors were
   told: "Do not kill,
for anyone who kills will have to be judged."
But I tell you that anyone
   who gets angry with his brother
he will have to be judged.*

After we had read this verse there was a long
silence. Since nobody spoke I asked Tomás
Peña: "What do you say, Tomás?"

He answered: "I'm thinking it over."

After another long pause, TOMÁS said: "I see
that there are two commandments in one. The
first time was only do not kill. Now it's two in
one: Do not kill, and do not hate your friend
either. We shouldn't do either. And I think it's
better now than the first law they had. Because Jesus doesn't want us to live with bad
feeling for anybody. Let's all live like brothers

and sisters, then, peaceful. Helping each other. You see? And let hatred stop."

And I commented: "It's not enough for us not to kill each other, is it? To live happily we must live like brothers and sisters, as Tomás says, that is, without hatred."

TOMÁS: "And the person who lives in hatred will never be able to live in peace. He has to be fighting with a list of enemies. And if he hates, he will also be hated. And if there are quarrels, there can also be murders. And Jesus wants, then, to put an end to all fighting, to put an end to the root of evil."

MANUEL: "Well, it's a stricter law, right? More screwed up, you know what I mean? Because hell! the law of Moses used to forbid only killing. Now it's not only that the guy who kills is condemned but the guy who gets angry with his brother. The whole thing is more complicated."

OLIVIA: "It's nicer. It's just that we have to understand this new law very well. Because it's better for us. It's not more screwed up, it's better. Because there are people who say: 'Hell, I haven't killed nobody, I haven't sinned.' And there are so many injustices committed against your neighbor that are like killing. And the root of these injustices is lack of love for our neighbor. And that's why the law of Jesus Christ is the law of love. I don't think it's more screwed up."

196

MANUEL: "Well, yes, of course it's better, but more difficult to obey."

OLIVIA: "Maybe because we don't want to, but if we're intelligent we can live a life of love for all. It's just if you want to."

MANUEL: "And who doesn't want to be saved, Doña Olivia? What happens is that . . . well, you get screwed up."

OLIVIA: "Well, when you really want to be saved, everything is easy. But if you don't, the laws are difficult. I don't find them at all difficult. What happens is that if we're selfish, everything is difficult. If we're not selfish, it's easy to help others, and it's even a pleasure. And it's easy to forgive others. Or to understand. It's the logical way that we ought to be treating each other, as brothers and sisters."

I said: "Israel had the commandment against killing, and nevertheless there were many murders in Israel, because it was a society filled with injustice and oppression. Jesus wants us to have a society in which there is no hatred or scorn or offense against anyone, that is, no injustice, and only in this way can we have a society without crimes. It's also for that very reason that Saint John says later that someone who hates his brother is a murderer (that is a way of saying that someone who commits injustices is a murderer)."

TOMÁS: "The trouble is that we don't understand each other. Maybe when we're on the up and up, as the saying goes, we can say we're brothers and sisters. And maybe we love each other. But when we start drinking liquor, we act crazy and then the trouble begins. Even though you don't want to, at times the rum itself makes you misunderstand, and then you get in a fight."

One of the boys said to him: "But that must be because you already had hatred in your heart."

TOMÁS: "Maybe not sometimes. Because I've seen that maybe some who are close pals, who give each other cigarettes, give this or that, are getting along fine, you know? But after some rum, one little word . . . "

Another of the boys: "False friends, Don Tomás?"

TOMÁS: "No, because I've watched some of them and it's clear that they like each other. But at those times, one swallow, two swallows, and that's it. One says to the other: You're a son-of-a-so-and-so. Maybe because the other guy respected him, he didn't say anything. But after a while the other one says something, with more rum, and he contradicts him, you see, and there you are. . . . I think drinking rum is the most dangerous thing for us here on earth."

One of the girls: "For the people. Let's say for the poor, because the rich get slaughtered in a different way."

TOMÁS: "But if one of them commits a crime nothing happens to him. He pays and gets off free. But not us. Whether we punch somebody or if somebody punches us. Maybe the fellow that got punched is sick because he doesn't have anything to take care of himself with, and the other fellow's in jail because he doesn't have any way to get out of jail. In any case, we all lose."

A man who insults his brother
will be judged by the Supreme Tribunal;
and a man who calls his brother an idiot
is in danger of hell's fire.

I said that the Supreme Tribunal, or *Sanhedrin*, was the highest authority of the Jews. As for what is here translated as "hell's fire," it is something that Christ called in his language *"Gehenna* of fire." *Gehenna* was the rubbish heap of Jerusalem, and as they were accustomed to burn the rubbish, there were often fires there. In the time of Christ, *Gehenna* already meant also a place of punishment in the other life, what we call hell. It's hard to know if Christ here is really referring to hell or if it's only a way of speaking.

And ÓSCAR said: "I imagine that, since our Jerusalem must be a city of love, anyone who hates cannot be in it. Anyone who can't get along with his neighbors gets shoved out, like rubbish, like Ge . . . what did you call it? Well, like something useless."

"And the fire is for everything useless," added ANDREA, his wife.

TOMÁS: "Maybe somebody that says 'idiot' is more of an idiot than the fellow he's talking to—right?—because he doesn't understand him. And it also seems to me that a guy who calls somebody an idiot doesn't realize the insult that's in the word 'idiot' and so he's a fool to say it."

I said: "But the greatest insult to our neighbor is exploitation—keeping people in an inferior social class . . . "

And FELIPE added: "They think that poor people are animals, they treat them like animals, and they give them no education."

DANIEL: "And the boss is always yelling at the workers, calling them idiots, and the workers have to put up with it."

ROSITA: "But we're used to that word 'idiot' in our homes: 'Where is that idiot'?"

DANIEL: "Christ is referring to another way of using it. It's when the boss says to the worker: 'You're an animal!' or when he says to him: 'Imbecile!' It's not like saying it informally or among friends."

I said: "Jesus is referring here to any insult said to a brother and he gives this word as a simple example. But he doesn't mean that we can't use it or that we can use it only informally. With the Pharisees he used very similar words. He often called them 'blind and stupid' (in addition to 'hypocrites' and 'race of vipers')."

And so if you take your offering to the altar
and there you remember that
    your brother has a quarrel with you,
leave your offering right there
    before the altar
and go first to make your peace
    with your brother.
Then you can return to the altar
    and make your offering.

TOMÁS: "It seems to me that these offerings at the temple were like a thing that one goes to give with love. For instance, if I was going to the temple and I was not friendly with a certain person and I was still going to give the offering, then I wouldn't be doing anything, like a person who is not going to give with love but just not to be left out. It seems to me that that's the way we should understand what he says about offerings."

OLIVIA: "Those offerings could be to beg forgiveness for sins, but Jesus says that you have to beg the forgiveness of the offended person before you ask for God's forgiveness. Or the offerings could be to please God, but if I'm filled with hate, God is not grateful to me. The love we have for each other, that's the best offering we can make to God."

I said: "The Jews believed in these sacrifices in the temple, and Jesus here is not telling them not to make them but that first they must have love among themselves. But later Jesus gradually taught them that those sacrifices were unnecessary, and that the only sacrifice that pleases God is love for others, and later on his disciples totally eliminated sacrifices. Saint Paul says that serving others and living with possessions in common are the sacrifices that please God."

JULIO RAMÓN: "And what can we say then of all those celebrations that the rich have in the churches? They ought to stop them, because God is not interested in that."

ADÁN: "Only when there is a reconciliation in society and an end to all exploitation and class division, only then can there be a true offering to God, right?"

TOMÁS: "Yes."

I: "That's why Father Camilo Torres believed that to celebrate an authentic Eucharist he had to fight first for social change."

FELIPE: "For the community of property."

> *If someone sues you and takes you to court,*
> *come to an agreement with him on the way,*
> *so he won't turn you over to the judge;*
> *because if he does,*
> *the judge will turn you over to the police*
> *and they will put you in jail.*
> *In truth I say to you*
> *that you will not get out of there*
>   *until you pay the last cent.*

MANUEL: "That also is reconciliation."

OLIVIA: "It's like Tomás said, because if two

poor people fight it makes business for the authorities. It means that love and harmony are very good for the poor. Because, look, each lawsuit means money that they'll take away from you, until you pay the last cent. They'll take all they want away from you."

TOMÁS: "And if you don't have it you'll have to go looking for it. Go in debt with the boss. The guy that does that is in for trouble. He doesn't go to jail but he'll have to figure out how to pay. In the long run he's maybe worse off than the fellow who's in jail."

RAÚL: "He's telling us not to be saps, that if the laws are repressive, it's better for us to settle things among ourselves and not fall under the forces of repression."

I: "This has a lot to do with the reality of our present system, and it also had meaning in the time of Christ. But it seems to me that he is not referring to this reality but giving us a parable."

RAÚL: "But here he's talking about the judge and the police and jail . . . "

DONALD, a young man who is studying in a little town in Costa Rica and has come home to spend the vacation, said: "In a revolutionary system there are also judges and police and jails."

OLIVIA: "So then I understood it right."

RAÚL: "Right. That's the way it is."

OLIVIA: "I understood it right."

RAÚL: "He's talking to the exploiters, and it's as if we already have revolutionary tribunals, then."

FELIPE: "To every unjust person he's saying that he ought to work things out as good as he can."

RAÚL: "If everyone followed the advice that he's just given we wouldn't need any revolutionary tribunals, then."

JULIO RAMÓN: "We're not going to need police or judges or anything."

MANUEL: "We won't need them. Yes, in a just society there's no need for any repression."

I said: "Because then there will only be love among brothers. But earlier Jesus said that every offense will be punished as murder was punished under the law of Moses. He spoke of hatred, insults, and scorn towards brothers. And he ended by saying to the oppressors that they better come to an understanding with their victims in time when they see that they are going to sue them."

RAÚL: "Because if they don't they get shot."

I: "They get shot or they go to hell. Jesus doesn't make it very clear if he's referring to punishments in this life or in the next one. First he spoke of the punishment of the *Sanhedrin*, which is an earthly punishment, and afterwards he spoke of *Gehenna*, which had an otherwordly meaning. Perhaps he wanted to leave it unclear so that we could interpret it as we wished. Or perhaps he is referring to the two punishments at the same time."

DONALD: "I don't know why, but that business of having to pay 'to the last cent' sounds to me as though we'll have to pay also in the next life."

GLORIA: "If the capitalists did what he says there'd be no need of a violent change."

ADÁN: "But the deal with the poor man has to be an honest one."

RAÚL: "That is, repay the victim with love, right?"

24.

Jesus Teaches How To Pray

(MATTHEW 6:7–15)

We read the passage where Jesus teaches his disciples to pray, with the words that have traditionally been called the "Our Father." First he warned them:

When you pray,
do not talk a lot, like pagans,
who with all their words
think they are going to be listened to.

I said that the translation is rather: "Don't go blah-blah-blah-blah like the pagans." For the Greek word that Matthew uses is *battalogein,* which is like saying "blah-blah-blah-blah."

WILLIAM: "It seems to me that if Christ tells them not to pray like pagans it's because the Jews prayed like pagans. And somewhere else Christ throws it in the Pharisees' faces that they said long prayers. And I think the same thing can be said of the Christians, that they pray like pagans, because the way they pray is

206

like the Jews and the other religions. Jesus' criticism is very serious, because it's condemning the customary way of praying in all religions, and he classifies it as pagan. And about the people that are considered religious he says that they don't know God or have any idea of what God is, which means they're pagans. And then he's going to teach a different way of praying, which will be very revolutionary."

I said also that, according to Saint Augustine, Christ didn't want to teach the Our Father as a formula that would be learned by heart. And proof of this is that in Matthew and in Luke the words are different, and if he had wanted to teach them a formula we would have to say that they didn't learn it very well.

We went on to comment on the first words:

Our Father who are in heaven.

Some further clarifications were necessary. I said that Jesus really didn't use the word "Father" but "Papa." Mark tells us what Jesus said in Aramaic (his mother tongue) in the prayer in the garden: *Abba*, which is "papa," and that was probably the word he always used in speaking of God. "Who are in heaven" is a Jewish way of meaning God. Out of respect they often didn't say the word "God" but the word "heaven," and so Matthew calls the kingdom of God the kingdom of heaven. Here the translation is rather: "Our heavenly papa," and what it means is "Our papa, God."

OLIVIA: "It's a loving name that's given to God. And from the very beginning we don't have to be formal when we chat with him and we give him the name of papa. So then to pray isn't to recite prayers but to chat with him."

TERESITA: "If we call him papa, there's no fear. We're on close terms with him."

WILLIAM: "That business of calling the kingdom of God the kingdom of heaven has led to a lot of confusion. Because people have believed that the kingdom will be in heaven, in the next life, but Christ was talking of a kingdom here on earth. And also to say 'who are in heaven' has created an awful confusion in our minds too. Because we imagine the Father as someone way up there where the astronauts are, instead of somebody who is inside you and in our other brothers."

JULIO: "And if the Jews out of respect for God didn't say the name of God and Christ himself doesn't want to mention it either, wouldn't it be good for us too not to be using the word 'God'? Because Christians are always saying God, God, God, and that's like a blasphemy because they're thinking of a dictator. But there are others that maybe are atheists but they love their brothers and I believe that they're showing respect for God."

And REBECA, his mother: "But Jesus teaches us to call him 'papa' so we won't feel he's far away. And he doesn't say 'My Father' or 'My papa' but 'our,' because he's the Father of us all. We're all his children, not only Christ but all of us. And therefore we're all brothers."

NATALIA: "Brothers. When we talk to God like that we're declaring that we're all equal. And we have to love each other like the children of the same papa. And if somebody thinks there should be exploiters, he can't pray that way."

MARCELINO, Rebeca's husband: "The Our Father is a community prayer, of all of us, and we're supposed to pray in community. And what we ask for is for everybody."

Holy be your name.

I explained that for the Jews "God" was the same as saying holiness or justice. And holiness was the sign of God among us. "Name" for them was the same as saying "person," or also, as we now say, "personality." This petition "holy be your name," might better be translated as: "May your person be made known." Or: "May you be acknowledged (doing justice)."

FELIPE PEÑA: "To make something holy then doesn't mean to chant, to say prayers, to have processions, to read the Bible. Making the name of God holy means to love others, to do something for others. If we set to glorifying God just with prayers and processions as we used to, we're not making God holy at all. In other words to make love real is to make the name of God holy or to make his person known here on earth, even though maybe the name of God won't even be mentioned."

ALEJANDRO: "God's justice is the same as his holiness and to make justice real means to make holy. But by justice we can't mean bourgeois justice. Justice is the same as liberation, to put an end to all exploitation, and that means to make God known, to reveal him among ourselves."

May your kingdom come.

LAUREANO: "This kingdom that we hope for will come when there's equality, when there's brotherhood. We here *do* want the kingdom to come. We're building it."

TOMÁS: "If we ask for it to come it means it hasn't come. And if we ask for it to come it means it has to come. And if it has to *come* it's not heaven or the next life. We don't ask for that to come, we ask to go there. So this must be a thing that has to come to the earth and that hasn't come yet. That's the way it seems to me, though I don't know much about it."

LAUREANO: "If we ask for it we're obliged to do everything we can to make this kingdom come. And they have no right to talk, people who are against this kingdom or who aren't interested in it or who aren't doing anything to build it. Because it's a kingdom that's made among people and with people. I mean it comes from God but it can't be made without us."

ROSITA: "It's love."

ELVIS: "And this is a prayer, then, that forces us to act, like Laureano said."

I added that this petition is really the same as the first one.

And we went on to the following one:

May your will be done
on earth as it is done in heaven.

OLIVIA: "In heaven they live a life of love, there's no selfishness there. And there aren't any injustices or oppressions either. Here we live in a very different way. In this prayer we're asking to live here like they live there. We have a long way to go before we see that kingdom built here. Here some people are starving to death and others waste food. Some sick people have no way to get cured and others have more medical attention than they need. Some people have too many clothes and others don't have a single change. So that means that it will take a lot of work to see this kingdom come. It will take ... "

"May what's done in heaven be done on earth is like saying let heaven be made on earth," said TERESITA.

"The will of God is love," said one of the Guevara girls.

And I said that we see then that this is the same petition as the others too: Let God's love be revealed among people, let his kingdom come, which is the kingdom of love, let God's will be done, which is love ...

FELIPE: "May your will be done also means may your teachings be fulfilled. That is, may justice be done. The creation of a just system, of equality and companionship, and not of exploitation. In other words, may the word of God be fulfilled. This is the same petition as for bread: that we all have enough."

MANUEL ALVARADO: "Bread and all the things that Doña Olivia was talking about: clothes, medicines, and all the other things that we need. It seems to me that the word 'bread' means all that."

Give us today the bread that we need.

JULIO MAIRENA: "And wouldn't Christ consider everything like a single day? Because he says give us the bread *today*, for this day. Could it be that all days are for him a single day?"

JULIO was asked to make himself clearer, and he said: "Not the way we say 'tomorrow' or 'the day after tomorrow' but that for him everything is a single day. Because if we're going to be asking today for now, and tomorrow for tomorrow. . . . I think he meant to say for all time."

LAUREANO, his cousin: "But are you going to be asking for a whole mess of it just to store it up, you ass?"

JULIO, laughing: "Because it'll go bad, won't it?"

OLIVIA: "Be careful. It seems to me that if God gave me a whole lot of things, I'd think I'd never need anything again. And so I wouldn't think about God anymore, because I'm

212

stuffed. I wouldn't remember other people or care about anybody else. You ask him every day because you ask him like you ask your papa, like the little boy that asks every day. And you ask him for enough. Not as if we lived just on bananas."

JULIO: "As I see it we have just one job to do. To change society and to have bread that day: for all time. For every day. Once and for all. That's what I find. If we're always going to be begging for a little bit of bread, today for today, and tomorrow and the day after tomorrow . . . that way we'd always be in need. No: we'll just do the job once and afterwards we'll always have enough to eat and enough to wear and all the rest. That's what I meant when I said that Jesus wasn't really talking about a single day . . . "

RAFAEL: "I think what Julio says is quite right. Let it be forever, right? But it's also clear that it's not a question of storing it up, as Laureano says, but we have to ask just for what we need and not what somebody else might need for today, you see?"

And REBECA, the mother of Óscar and Julio: "As I see it, God gives bread every day. He gives every day for everybody. But at times the strongest one is the one that hoards and the one who can't, well, he's left hungry. God gives bread every day so we can all eat, so nobody will be left hungry."

MARCELINO: "We ask for *our* bread and not my bread, like we used to call God our papa and

213

not my papa. To ask for our bread is to ask for it for everybody and for nobody to be left hungry either today or tomorrow."

I said: "That's the same petition as the earlier ones: Let the kingdom of love come and the day when there's an abundance of bread for everybody."

NATALIA: "Yes, enough for everybody. When nobody has too much and nobody dies of hunger, that's the kingdom."

JULIO said, laughing: "Then let's go ask for it from those who have it hoarded up. Let's ask for it from those who have too much. Our duty is to take it away from them, because they have what's not their share. They have extra and it belongs to the people who are in need."

I: "We might say then that here we're asking for change to occur. The day when we can distribute to everybody, according to their needs, the things that are now monopolized. And we see that it's not only up to us to beg for this change but to bring it about."

REBECA: "It's liberation, so we'll all be equal, and there won't be no poor and there won't be no rich."

"The kingdom of God," added someone.

And REBECA: "The kingdom of God, which is liberation."

FELIPE: "This means the will of God has been done."

ÓSCAR: "I also understand, Ernesto, that

214

when we ask him for bread and the other things we need, we have to fight to get them, as we've said, not only for ourselves but for the others. But until the time we can get them, we have to put up with things, because that also may be the will of God for the moment."

"No!" interrupted LAUREANO. "That's being a conformist."

And Óscar's mother: "That's going along with exploitation."

ÓSCAR continued: "Let me explain: It's not to accept exploitation but to accept the will of God. I see it this way, look, if we as a group are opposed to injustice and if we're struggling and we can't get what we want, if we can't bring about the change for the time being, well, let his will be done. But we don't lie down! We have to keep moving ahead."

I told Óscar that we do have to accept the defeat that's beyond our control. We must not rebel against what's unavoidable but only against what's avoidable. And sometimes good can come out of defeat. And in that sense failure can be the will of God. We have to remember that this was Jesus' prayer on the Mount of Olives, when he faced his own failure, the same prayer that he had taught his disciples. According to Mark his prayer went: "*Abba* (Papa), may your will be done."

OLIVIA: "His will, after all, must be for us to live. His will must be for us to have happiness, not disasters. So we should be able to accept our own suffering, and even be happy with it."

215

Forgive us our debts,
as we forgive our debtors.

OLIVIA: "There's where we have to have that acceptance Óscar speaks of, because if anyone offends us it's out of ignorance. And if that guy offended me that's no reason to offend him."

I: "We shouldn't have hatred or bitterness or any negative feeling, right?"

REBECA: "I believe we have to beg God's forgiveness for our sins, which are selfishness. It wouldn't do us any good to be begging his pardon if we kept on being selfish. We have to change our attitude if he's going to hear us. And that's why we ask him to forgive us and say that we forgive."

WILLIAM: "Because we saw that the kingdom of God was the kingdom of love. As long as there's selfishness this kingdom won't come. And there won't be bread for everybody as long as there's selfishness, fights among us, and we don't love each other. And it wouldn't do any good for all of us to have food and clothing and all we need if there's bitterness and hatred among us. Right? So there has to be love among us all."

ÓSCAR: "If there isn't, there won't be any kingdom either."

FELIPE: "And the will of God won't be fulfilled, which is what's happening now."

COSME CANALES: "We say we forgive those who are in debt to us; that can mean any of-

216

fense. But it can also mean money debts. I
don't say we shouldn't ask for payment of a
debt if the guy can pay, but if he can't, we
ought to forgive him. For a lot of rich people
it's easier to forgive an offense, any offense,
than to forgive a debt."

ROSITA: "Did you ever see a rich person forgive
a debt?"

COSME continued: "And so a rich person can't
say this prayer if he isn't ready to forgive not
just offenses but debts, too."

CHAEL: "We know of course that this prayer is
not for the rich. The Our Father is only for the
poor, for those who have no bread."

I said that, in the new liturgical reforms, the
old translation "Forgive us our debts as we
forgive our debtors" was changed to "Forgive
us our offenses as we forgive those who offend
us." But the first translation was the correct
one, for Matthew used a Greek word that
means exactly a money debt, the same word
that he must have used a lot in his job as a
publican, or tax collector.

And do not put us to the test
but free us from evil.

JULIO RAMÓN: "By 'do not put us to the test' I
understand that he means not to put us in
competition. Who with? It must be with the
devil, I think."

ADÁN ORTEGA: "The test now, I believe, is exploitation, capitalism."

And the other JULIO: "I think that we who are talking here talk a lot about change. Maybe we'll be put to the test some day, if we're lucky enough to have enough power. It's a test that could be very hard."

TOMASITO (who says very little): "Free us from evil means free us from injustice. Something like that, I think ... "

FELIPE: "And in other words free us from evil is free us from selfishness. It's the greatest evil that can exist among us, selfishness. Anybody who controls other people, it's because he's selfish. Anybody who steals is selfish. That's why we have to ask God to free us from selfishness. That's the evil. Now, love is the opposite of evil. Evil is defeated by love. That's the only thing stronger than evil, love."

JULIO MAIRENA: "Jesus said that we don't need to pray with a lot of words because God knows what we need. Then we don't need to pray with just a few words, either, because he already knows. I think the formal prayers that are chanted in church are pagan prayers. I bet you God doesn't want us to pray to him but to act instead."

I said that Christ didn't tell us not to pray, but just not to pray asking for a lot of things like the pagans, because the Father knows what we need. He used to pray, and Luke tells us he taught this prayer because the disciples, who had watched him praying, asked him to teach them to pray. And what do you suppose his prayer was? I'm sure it must have been this one, because it's the one he taught.

LAUREANO: "It seems to me that the few little words that he taught, these words, take in almost everything. And that's why he tells us not to pray with a lot of words, blah-blah-blah like the pagans. There's no reason to be asking for pants, shirts, shoes, because it's all included in this prayer for change."

REBECA: "We ask for love to rule. That way all evil comes to an end."

I said that we see that all these petitions are really a single prayer, the prayer of liberation: for his name to be revealed, which is this liberation (which is also the name of Jesus); for his kingdom of love to come; for his will to be done, which is love; for there to be bread for all; for him to forgive us in our forgiveness of others, since we've offended him in others, and among ourselves for nobody to owe anything to anyone else; and finally for him to free us from all injustice.

NATALIA: "A kingdom of brotherhood, with justice, with bread, with forgiveness, with love. This covers everything."

JULIO: "And so isn't to say a lot of Our Fathers to pray like pagans?"

WILLIAM said: "We pray to God for his name to be holy, and it's up to us to make his name holy. We pray for his kingdom to come, and it's up to us to build it. We pray that his will be done on earth, and it's up to us to do his will. We pray to him for bread, and it's up to us to make it and share it. We pray to him for forgiveness, and it's up to us to forgive. We pray not to fall into evil and it's up to us to escape from it. That's what's interesting about this prayer. I think that a lot of people maybe don't say the Our Father, like Che didn't say it, but in their hearts they're asking for all this."

I said that this is the prayer we should have. That it's the one that Christ said on earth, and the one that, according to Saint Paul, he goes on saying in our hearts. I ended by reading what the Letter to the Galatians (4:6) says: "As we are his sons, God sent into our hearts the Spirit of his Son, crying: '*Abba*, Papa!' "

25.

"Look at the Lilies in the Field . . ."

(MATTHEW 6:24–34)

We were gathered in our little church with the dirt floor. With us were the poets José Coronel Urtecho and Pablo Antonio Cuadra, who had come to spend a few days with us. And also our friend Samuel (a painter who had recently been changing into a financier) and a South American friend of his who is a Vice President of the Inter-American Development Bank (IDB) in New York had come in a small plane from Managua to spend a few hours with us. The Gospel passage that we were to comment on that Sunday was that of the lilies in the field.

No one can serve two masters,
because he will hate one and love the other,
or he will be faithful
  to one and despise the other.
You cannot serve God and money.

REBECA: "Because money makes you selfish, hardens you, keeps you from loving."

Young GLORIA: "Money isolates people. It separates them from others. I mean the love of money."

And JOSÉ ESPINOSA, a middle-aged *campesino:* "Love for money makes you proud. You want to excel over others, to be more than the other fellow, and that's why people get split up into classes."

I asked: "Then according to this verse you can't be a Christian and be rich?"

Young LAUREANO, who always gave very radical answers: "He's condemning the rich completely."

Old TOMÁS, slowly: "It seems to me that he wasn't. If he said that, he meant you can't belong to two classes."

DON CHON: "It seems to me that he's condemning them. Yes, because we can't give. What we have is scarcely enough for ourselves, and if maybe we do give it's a little thing. We can't give much because we don't have much. Yet they get all the breaks because they're the ones who have it."

And FÉLIX, who when the rich are attacked often comes to their defense (although he's as poor as the rest): "He said 'serve,' he didn't say 'be rich.' There are rich people who aren't servants of money but use it to do good for others, although there aren't many rich people like that."

COSME CANALES, the boatman: "They aren't rich any more. They were rich and now they're poor, because they used their money to serve their neighbor."

OLIVIA: "The rich can be saved when they stop being rich."

ÓSCAR: "I say this, see. If he uses money to help, he can be a Christian. But if he has it only to go on hoarding it, no. Because money is also useful if I, as a rich man, distribute it to the people. Even though money by itself is worth nothing. In God's eyes money is worth nothing, hoarded in the form of capital, but money is valuable to God when it's used for something good."

I: "Really the Gospel is talking about serving money ... "

And ÓSCAR went on: "Well, it seems to me that serving money, as Jesus says there, is to be keeping it and increasing it, making the capital bigger."

LAUREANO: "That's what the rich do. There's no rich person that gives his money away, because then he'll be poor."

GLORIA: "Well, the best thing is to have no rich people."

EDUARDO (to Óscar): "That's what you say right now, but if you had money you'd want more and when you had more you'd want even more."

ÓSCAR: "I think there are some people with money who are good, open-hearted people. Those are Christians. There are others who give only what they can't use and that's not being a Christian."

MARÍITA: "I think you can't be a Christian if you're ruled by love of money, but you *can* be a Christian when you've given it away. That means you can't serve two bosses at the same time. Any millionaire can be a Christian, but only when he's given his money away to the poor."

WILLIAM: "To serve means to love, and what Christ is saying is that you can't love God and love money. Because God is love and love of money is selfishness."

FÉLIX: "Then Jesus doesn't condemn just the rich but everyone who is greedy for money even though he's very poor."

"Of course."

"And the day when there's no rich people and there's no poor people greedy for money, then all of us are going to be able to serve God," said DOÑA ÁNGELA.

I said that the word that Christ used here to refer to money is the Aramaic word *Mammon*, which is the name of the God of wealth, an idol, and he was making us see that the love of money is idolatry.

The poet PABLO ANTONIO said: "The Greeks also deified money with the name of Pluto. I believe that cult has existed since money was invented. But now the god of money is more of a god than ever."

And the poet CORONEL: "And the banks are his temples." And he said, turning to the Vice President of the IDB: "I've always been struck by bank architecture, which is so like that of temples . . . "

The VICE PRESIDENT: "And shouldn't we also understand the words of Christ in the context of the economy of the times, which was a slave system? That must be why he talks of two masters . . . "

CORONEL: "But as long as we are under the control of money we are part of a system of slavery, although the relations between masters and slaves are given another name today. Slavery is now in its capitalistic phase, but the slavery is more gigantic. I imagine the money that goes from hand to hand to be like a long, long chain that links everybody's neck together and winds up on Wall Street, which is where all the money ends, as you know. The *pesos* that you have in your wallet (fortunately I don't have any at the moment) don't belong to you. They belong to Wall Street. You can believe you've earned them and that they belong to you, but they'll go from hand to hand until they get to Wall Street. As these revolutionary faithful have made clear to us here, to serve money is to serve slavery, while to serve the opposing master is to be free."

And ÓSCAR said: "It's obvious that if you have capital you don't have love."

And WILLIAM said: "You can't have love and selfishness at the same time. That's why love and money are incompatible."

And FELIPE: "And it's clear that if you want to serve others, you don't want money. And if it's money that interests you, you don't want to serve others. That's why he says that if you love one you despise the other. In other words love of neighbor is incompatible with love of money."

I say to you then:
Do not worry about what you
   are going to eat or drink to stay alive,
nor about the clothes
   that you are going to wear.
Isn't life worth more than food,
and the body worth more than clothes?
Look at the birds in the sky,
that do not sow or reap or have granaries;
yet your Father in heaven feeds them.
How much more valuable you are
   than the birds!
And which of you,
no matter how much you worry about it,
can make yourself a half-yard taller?

ADÁN: "He says we should look at the birds. One thing we can learn from them is that they

226

don't exploit each other. Among them there are no rich and no poor. They have no social classes."

JULIO MAIRENA: "And another thing we must learn from them is not to be weighed down by the future. God wants us to live free and easy like the birds. They don't have any harvests and they are free, so we should be much freer with the harvests and all the other things that we produce. They are animals and are not weighed down, so we who are the children of God should be weighed down even less."

Through the door and the two windows on one side of the church we can see the lake to the north, and through the door and the other two windows on the other side we can also see the lake on the south side. And through the open front, still unfinished, we see a green field filled with trees. I said that Christ invites us to look at this nature that surrounds us on all sides that we can see is all brimming with food: fish in the water, herons on the shore, iguanas in the trees, sparrows, flowers, grass, all beings find more than enough food, which serves as abundant food to other beings. For many, these are the blind forces of nature. Christ wants us to know that there is a great love that watches over us.

A lady who has come from the opposite shore (from the Valley of Guadalupe) said: "Well, as the mother of nine children I've always lived with that trust, and we've never had any money but we've never lacked what is necessary. Something always turns up. I'd never heard this Gospel, but it seems to me it's almost our lives."

REBECA: "God always works miracles."

DOÑA CHICA: "This Gospel is for people in trouble, poor people."

FELIPE: "I'm worried about one thing. Won't this Gospel alienate the poor even more? Because you can go up to a poor woman, one of those mothers who sell things in the market, for example, and say to her, 'Don't you worry, ma'am. Maybe tomorrow your onions will bring a better price, have faith ... ' "

GUSTAVO: "But Felipe, I want to ask you something. For example, you go to that lady and you tell her, 'Come with your husband and we're going to go to work to change this system.' And she says to you, 'No, no, because I have some onions that I have grown.' Are you going to say, 'Is your harvest more important than solving all the world's problems?' Of course you won't. You'll say, 'Don't worry about that, we'll find a way to settle things, and let's fight to change things.' Right?"

FELIPE: "Yes, of course."

ALEJANDRO: "I don't know, I believe in miracles and all that, but when the Gospel asks us not to worry, I see clearly that it's talking about a social change. That is, it's not a question just of waiting around for miracles. The thief often steals because his family has nothing to eat, and he lives with that worry. And the rich person worries about making more money. I believe we can have a social system in which we don't have that worry, that anguish that I'm going to lose my job or have less money than the other fellow or that I'll get sick or what am I going to do when I'm old. But not in this other system, because you have all you need and nobody's going to take it away from you and you can devote yourself to working in peace, to studying and all that, without that desperation."

GUSTAVO: "But I believe that on the road to that system, which can be a very long road, it's more necessary than ever to have that lack of concern. Because when you work for other people you maybe won't have any support. You're going to be up in the air, and if you don't have that confidence that Jesus talks about, you won't dare take a step. You'll just stick to your personal interests, to your selfish concerns. That's what happens to middle-class people. Middle-class worries are always stupid, because they are unreal like that example that Jesus gives of wanting to be a half-yard taller; and besides being unreal they are useless, because what good does it do you to be taller than the others?"

And why do you worry about clothes?
Look at how the flowers grow in the fields;
they do not work or spin,
and nevertheless I say to you
that not even King Solomon

with all his luxury
was dressed like one of them.
And if God dresses the wild grass this way,
grass that today is in the field
and tomorrow is burned in the oven,
how much more will he do for
you men of little faith!

One of the young men said: "You ought to dress any way you want. You shouldn't go around worrying about clothes. It seems to me that's what Christ means."

And another, LAUREANO, said: "But if you don't dress nice the girls don't like you."

There were titters and laughter among the girls. Afterwards GLORIA said: "It's clear that Jesus here had no admiration for kings or for riches. Because Solomon must have dressed with great luxury and Jesus preferred a little wild flower over all that luxury."

And ALEJANDRO: "When the new social system comes we'll all be dressed better than King Solomon. Because we don't like those luxurious clothes, we don't think that is dressing well."

OLIVIA: "The grass is very pretty but it soon passes, while human beings are destined for eternal life. And therefore all these material things are very important, even clothes, as Laureano says. But to be concerned only about yourself is to have little faith, not to believe in the kingdom of God. Christ doesn't tell us not to spin, not to harvest, . . . but not to do it only for our own sakes, looking out only for our own food, our own clothing, instead of working for others."

JULIO: "Look at the flowers, look at the birds, Jesus tells us. Because we can have many wrong ideas because we don't notice the material world."

Therefore do not worry saying:
"What are we going to eat?"
or "What are we going to drink?"
or "What are we going to
*   clothe ourselves with?"*
Because the pagans toil for all these things;
but you have a heavenly Father
who knows that you need all that.

I said: "We must remember that the pagans that Christ talks about were very religious, and their religiosity was precisely to ask for rain, fertility, good harvests. Just like there is among us a popular religiosity very similar to that. And it seems to me that Christ is saying that we do not need a religion to ask for those things because the Father already knows that we need them."

WILLIAM: "And there is another part of the Gospel where Christ says that God makes it rain upon good people and bad people. Even more we can say that he makes it rain on people who pray and on people who don't pray. But there is a love that rules the universe, and it's important to know that."

MARCELINO: "It doesn't mean don't work, but

don't worry about it. The plant works sucking the juice from the earth, it doesn't sleep. We should follow the example of the flower in the field, that works, and of the corn that works. The corn that we sow doesn't say, 'All right, now I'm not going to grow and I'm not going to do anything.' "

FRANCISCO: "There's a lot of selfishness among the poor. I think we're poor because we are selfish."

JOSÉ ESPINOSA: "No, those who exploit us are the selfish ones. Even though we work we're poor. I sowed a rice field and it came up fine and the price is awful. The businessmen set the price of what we sell in San Carlos. And also of what we buy."

PABLO ANTONIO: "And those fellows have their prices set by others, and that's the chain."

MANUEL: "We sowed two acres of rice and we got only one acre out of it, and it's not because we didn't work hard, because we did. You work, but it does you no good."

FÉLIX: "You have to accept the will of God. Rice gives us very little. It's the will of God that we have little. They pay us badly in San Carlos. It's the will of God that we stay poor."

JOSÉ ESPINOSA: "No, the will of God is that we fight, and he's going to fight at our side."

MARCELINO: "And that's why we must seek the kingdom of God and his justice."

The IDB man said: "I am a vice president of a foreign bank with a lot of money, and I have listened to all this dialogue with great interest. What do you think that bank ought to do with its money, according to this Gospel?"

MARCELINO: "It's very clear: Give it out."

The IDB man: "Give it out? That's very easy. But then there won't be any money to lend to people in need."

MARCELINO: "You have to give the money out, but you can't take it back again. Because those who have the money can give it away, but since they are very powerful, they can take it back. And they take back more than they've given away, and the poor are then left poorer than before. But if they give it away and don't take it back then there won't be any more poor people."

The poet PABLO ANTONIO said: "Let's make no mistake. It's Christ who is talking with the voice of the *campesinos* of Solentiname. To be sure it is a very *campesino* passage, this one about the lilies in the field. I imagine that Christ must surely have spoken in the middle of a field, as we are here, and maybe with that lake of his opposite him, like this one. And he was talking for *campesinos* with economic problems very similar to those of these people in Solentiname. He was a *campesino*, too. We feel in this passage that he is talking with the simplicity and the poetry of the *campesinos* of Galilee. Now he is talking with the poetry of the *campesinos* of Solentiname."

And our friend SAMUEL, who had come with his banker friend: "These words of Christ are very poetic but they can inspire very reactionary attitudes in us. Because in our environment to eliminate economic concerns means to eliminate progress. Would we return to the economy of primitive people? They were perhaps happy, but economic concerns, competition, ambition rightly understood (I call it initiative instead) have all been necessary for progress."

MARCELINO: "Initiative, good, to give to others, not to hoard for ourselves. And ambition to see that we all have enough and that nobody needs anything. And competition that I give to you and you give to me. For example: I give food and you give me clothes or shoes, and so neither of us has to worry about what we'll eat or what we'll wear."

CORONEL (to Samuel): "You are defending a modern system, which in the face of another more modern one turns out to be reactionary. The economic systems of the Gospels and of Marxism are both more modern than capitalism. It's a question of going back to the happiness of primitive people without the handicaps they would have as primitives. Besides, primitive people have been slandered a lot. Let's not forget the Altamira paintings. And right here we have the primitive painting of Solentiname that you admired this morning. Even so, in these poor and primitive conditions of Solentiname we can glimpse a new person."

SAMUEL: "I am not opposed to this Gospel. I've said that it's very fine. But I also see that, inspired by these fine words, we could ruin the economy . . . "

"The capitalist economy," said PABLO ANTONIO.

And CORONEL: "These very fine words would produce a very fine economy."

PABLO ANTONIO, smiling, to Samuel and his friend from the IDB: "The banks would be ruined."

CORONEL: "And the banks, as you know just as well as we do, are a great big shit."

So then, seek first
the kingdom of God and his justice,
and all the rest shall
be given to you in addition.

ÓSCAR: "I believe that the kingdom of God is unity, like we have here. And the happiness of being here. What more do we want? I feel very happy being here with everyone. For me that is the kingdom."

MARCELINO: "The kingdom of God is love. And justice, it's the same. Let's try to bring about this society of love and justice, and then there will be no more exploitation. And therefore there will be abundance for everybody. We'll all have not only food and clothing but also schools, clinics, hospitals, adequate housing, all we need."

MANUEL: "I'd like to give an example. In the country you could open a wonderful school, and not a single child comes. Why not? Because they have to work with their parents, and they have to take care of their homes and the little children. On the other hand if there's social justice, the schools will be put up almost all by themselves, and the children then would really be free to study. That is, all the rest shall be given in addition."

FELIPE: "God gives things to people like he gives them to the birds. And more than to the birds. He gives us the earth and all that we take out of the earth to eat and to clothe ourselves and to live in comfort. But people take things away from each other. Then some have and others don't. That's why, if we seek the kingdom of brotherhood and justice, we're going to have all the things that God gives."

GUSTAVO: "We'd already have reached the kingdom of God if it wasn't because most people devote themselves only to looking for their own economic security."

WILLIAM: "All the rest, comforts, material things, are not important. What's important is love. But that 'addition' is also necessary."

PABLO ANTONIO: "There are some who believe that the problem of social justice is going to be solved after economic development is solved. According to Jesus it's just the opposite."

I said: "It's often said also in the Church that before society is changed we must seek to change the heart of man. Christ says that first comes the kingdom and its justice, or the kingdom of justice, which is the same thing. He doesn't say that first we must seek religious conversion and all the rest shall be given in addition. Because it is proven that religious conversions do not put an end to a system of exploitation. On the contrary, religion can be used for more exploitation."

And LAUREANO: "The kingdom of God is justice. That is, our only concern must be justice, which is to bring about the Revolution."

And CORONEL: "The kingdom of heaven is upon the earth, it's clear, but we can't forget that there's also a heaven, or, as it is called, a something beyond death. If not, our vision is incomplete. We're myopic. The myopic person is someone who can't see far. The dogma of the resurrection of the flesh means that the Revolution does not end in this world, that communism goes on after death."

We have come to the end. And PABLO ANTONIO says to Coronel, sitting beside him: "Fidel would accept a Mass like this one. And it would have pleased Che."

26.

Do Not Cast Pearls to the Pigs

(MATTHEW 7:6–12)

*Do not give sacred things to the dogs
lest they turn against you
   and tear you to pieces.
And do not cast your pearls to the pigs
lest they tread on them.*

MANUEL said: "I think one of those sacred things is the Eucharist. There are people who receive sacred things without respecting them. They shouldn't be given to that kind of people."

JORGE: "And these people can attack you. If you give a hog jewels instead of corn the hog will get furious."

LAUREANO said: "I still don't get it."

QUIQUE: "Maybe it refers to people who think all government is sacred. People in authority are given what belongs to God, and they use power against the people."

238

LAUREANO (who was saying that he hadn't understood): "Each person is sacred. So it must be that you shouldn't exploit others and live off them."

DONALD: "I want to say something like what Laureano said. There are people in power who exploit others. The poor people get screwed and get exploited more and more, and they are looked down on as if they were garbage. So the hogs are the rich who are stepping on the pearls who are the workers."

ÓSCAR: "Maybe it's talking about the love that Christ came to bring to the earth. That's what's sacred, and also that's what the jewels are. And there are some people who are like dogs or pigs. You can't give them what's sacred, you can't give them the jewels."

DONALD: "Yes, sure, because if they're stepping on other people they're stepping on love."

FELIPE: "It seems to me that Jesus Christ calls people dogs who interpret the Gospels only to screw their neighbor, only to defend their interests. We can't give them this Gospel because then they'll just make use of it to exploit people."

QUIQUE: "Saying for example that the kingdom of heaven is going to be in heaven and that it has nothing to do with this world."

I said: "It seems, then, that according to Jesus the Gospel message must not be given to everyone because it's not for everyone."

FELIPE: "It seems to me that's it. All poor people have to agree with the Gospel because it's meant for their liberation. But this doesn't suit the middle class."

MANUEL: "But first we have to show them and try to explain to them."

FELIPE: "How are we going to preach liberation to someone who doesn't want liberation because he's an oppressor? There's no sense in talking to him about that."

OLIVIA: "It would be better instead for the exploiters not to hear these things. The Gospel is bound to make them furious and Christ knew this, and that's why he tells us to be careful."

Ask, and God will give to you;
seek and you will find;
knock at the door and it will open for you.

LAUREANO: "I believe that there he was referring to liberation, and the fulfillment of love among people. That's what we must ask for. And not just ask for. Because he also talks of knocking and seeking."

MANUEL: "He doesn't mean that we should pray and ask for anything we feel like and God is going to give it to us. Suppose I ask him for things that belong to someone else. He's not going to give them to me!"

Is there perhaps one of you
capable of giving a stone to your son
when he asks you for bread?
Or giving him a snake
when he asks you for a fish?

JORGE: "He's talking about good things. He's not referring to money. Because anybody who asks God to give him money is selfish. God won't grant that."

I said: "That must be like the son asking his father for a snake."

FELIPE: "It seems to me that the good things you can ask for are good ideas, good feelings toward your friends, a capacity for love. We'll always get all that if we ask for it."

So then always do unto others
as you want them to do unto you:
because this is the commandment
of the Law of Moses
and the Books of the Prophets.

FELIPE: "In other words: if we want other people to love us, we have to love them. And this can also mean that our liberation is involved in the liberation of others."

QUIQUE: "These are the good things Jesus says we should ask for and they will be given to us."

I said that Jesus was saying something very revolutionary here, and that it could even shock many religious people. By "the Law and the Prophets" Jesus means the whole Bible. And he says that the whole Bible, all it talks about is love for others. Not serving God, not worshiping God, not loving God, but doing unto others what we want them to do unto us. We might almost say that he makes an atheistic interpretation of the Bible.

QUIQUE: "He means that the guy who does

that is already obeying what the Bible says, even though he isn't religious, even though he says he doesn't believe in God. There are still a lot of people who think that the Bible, what it deals with is the relations between man and God, and according to Jesus that's not what it's all about. He takes religion away from the Bible and reduces it just to the relations between people."

I said there was a problem because right in Matthew (Chapter 22), when the Pharisees asked Jesus which was the most important commandment, he said it was to love God, and then he added that the second is very similar: to love your neighbor as yourself. And that these two commandments "are the basis of all the Law of Moses and the teachings of the prophets." Here, on the other hand, he doesn't talk of the love of God but only of love of others.

MANUEL: "Man! God is love itself. Why, somebody who loves God loves love itself. He loves his neighbor. It's all the same."

JORGE: "God is represented by humanity."

LAUREANO: "The two things say the same: Love God and love your neighbor as you love yourself. To do unto others what you want them to do unto you is to do good to them, and so that is to love God. It comes down to the same thing ... "

MANUEL interrupted: "And to love your neighbor is not merely to love God, it's the only way we have of loving God."

242

I said that Saint Paul had also said in the Letter to the Galatians that the whole Law is summed up in this single commandment: "Love your neighbor as yourself," in spite of the fact that Christ had earlier talked of two commandments. And it's because the love of God and the love of your neighbor are really the same, and anyone who loves his neighbor loves God. You can't say the opposite: that anyone who loves God has therefore fulfilled his duty to love his neighbor. Saint John said that somebody who loves only God and does not love his neighbor does not love God.

LAUREANO interrupts: "What the exploiters do is go to Mass and give alms in the church and pray and do all those drooly things with God, but with their neighbor: nothing. They just exploit him."

QUIQUE: "Those people really have no contact with God. They worship a false God, who does not exist."

FELIPE: "The one who loves God loves the people. You love God with deeds, not with your mouth."

I said that if loving God without love of your neighbor isn't loving God, and love of your neighbor without love of God really is the love of God, that means then that what counts is love of your neighbor.

JORGE: "If that's all the Bible says, then the Bible itself isn't what's important so much as loving your neighbor. And that's all we should ask for and look for."

MANUEL: "Loving your neighbor and being of service to him, because—watch it!—if all it is is love, you haven't done a thing."

I said: "It's doing for others what we want for ourselves. It's the same as saying loving your neighbor as yourself. Having consideration for others as for yourself, and for the people's cause as for the cause of each one of us. In reality all of us are a single organism, and all together we are a single I. That's why each one of us must love the others as a part of our own person (that means, "as oneself"). If we don't, we don't belong to the complete Man, we are cut off from humanity."

GLORIA: "And those who are cut off are like dogs and pigs. They are no longer people. And you can't say these truths to them because they don't understand them and they attack us."

27.

Jesus Announces the Persecutions

(MATTHEW 10:16–25)

*Look! I am sending you
like sheep in the midst of wolves.*

First OLIVIA spoke: "It seems to me that Jesus says this because the person who goes to preach his message goes with love, and preaches it in the midst of hatred. That's why they are like sheep among wolves. And people who don't accept the message can kill them."

TOMÁS PEÑA said: "I just want to say that I agree with what she said."

TERESITA: "There's a huge difference between people who belong to Jesus and people who don't, like the difference there is between love and hate."

And I: "The word 'wolf' we now use to talk about the exploitation of some people by others. It is man who becomes the devourer of his brother. So there is an enormous difference between some people and others, as if they were two very different species, the wolves and the lambs, when we are really all one species."

ÓSCAR: "And that species should be like lambs. Let's be as united and as peaceful as the lambs, I say."

Be, then, as sharp as serpents
but as harmless as doves.

LAUREANO: "At the same time he's telling us that we must be aggressive and peaceful. I understand it this way: When you have to use violence, use it, and when you can do things peacefully, do them peacefully. It's only a matter of tactics, I say."

ALEJANDRO: "There's a difference between being good and being a sap. Just because you're good you don't have to be an idiot, and Jesus is telling us here to be good without being idiotic—not letting anybody get ahead of you. Be sharp, sure! Watch out for the people's interests, and don't let anyone exploit them—that's to be as sharp as a serpent. And you can combine this with the methods of non-violence."

WILLIAM: "We must have the sharpness of the serpent without its evil, without its poison. That is, we must have the cunning of the enemy without his evil. In that way we must distinguish ourselves from him. Our goodness must be like the goodness of the doves."

Beware, because people
  will deliver you to the authorities
and they will beat upon you in the temples,
and they will even take you
  before governors and kings for my cause.

Someone else said: "And this is what we're seeing right now. Somebody in Nicaragua preaches Jesus' message without changing a word and he gets persecuted at once and can be jailed and they can even kill him."

And another one added: "He says they will be arrested for his cause. That cause is to struggle for social change, for everything he taught, even if you don't mention the name of Jesus. Because other people are always mentioning Jesus' name but they don't fight for his cause, and not a damn thing happens to them."

And another: "Of course, here he's talking about governments and he means that we're going to be accused of political crimes, of getting mixed up in politics, of being subversives, of being agitators. Because we don't go around shouting: 'Jesus loves us.' "

But when you are
  handed over to the authorities,
do not worry about what
  you are going to say
or how you are going to say it;
because when the moment comes to speak,
God will make the words come to you.
Because it will not be you that speak
but the Spirit of your Father
  that will speak in you.

One of the young people: "Usually when a person is accused for a just cause he's a very responsible person and the people that accuse him are usually very stupid. They're always stupid, always, because the tyrannical authorities, like the ones we have in Nicaragua, have to be like that. So you can always talk to them. With words you can crush them. So you don't even need to think of what you're going to say. The Spirit speaks through you, the conviction that you have, the faith in what you're doing. That's what it means."

Old TOMÁS PEÑA: "The person who knows the truth, the Christian, bothers the one who doesn't know and therefore the one who doesn't know the truth can even kill him . . . "

LAUREANO: "We have an example. When he was tried after the Moncada Barracks attack, Fidel gave a speech that left them flabbergasted. They couldn't even answer him. He accused them . . . "

Another: "That's what always happens when injustice persecutes justice."

Men will betray
their own brothers to be put to death
and fathers will betray their children;
children will turn against their parents
and will have them killed.

TOMÁS PEÑA: "We have to understand this. Because it's all explained here. Understand it and not do it. Not fall into the error of being the persecutors, but be Christians, that is, the persecuted."

And young ALEJANDRO: "We have to see this in practice. Let's not stay on the theory level. Let's see which are the times this happens in Solentiname, this split because of the Gospels. Let's not name names, but there are a lot of young people who have problems with their parents because of this, or with their older brothers and sisters, even with brothers and sisters who are almost their own age, with friends—friends that used to be friends and that now drop you to speak against you. And all this division is because you're on the side of the Gospels and the others aren't. The others are on the side of the system."

Old TOMÁS: "It's true, even in the same family. Maybe there are only three of us and one follows the Gospels and the other two don't, and the one can't persuade the other two and there's the split."

ALEJANDRO again: "We could point out cases, because we've seen them. We've had those cases."

His mother, OLIVIA: "And the same thing happens in the cities. And there are young people, boys and girls who have come here and because they've come here have had to break with their own families. Some maybe have been thrown out of their homes because they came to Solentiname, and maybe afterwards they'll never go back home. Egda was a girl who had problems at home because she came here and because she followed the Gospels."

Everyone will hate you for my cause;
but the one who remains
* steady until the end*
that one will be saved

ALEJANDRO: "And this really happens right now, too. There are people who shouldn't hate people who follow the Gospel. Because this Gospel is in their favor. But what happens is that these people have also been influenced by the propaganda of those on top, and they've persuaded them to be against their own interests, against their own class. And when a prophet, a redeemer, goes to them, they shoot at him. You can understand why the capitalists do that, because the Gospels are against capitalists. But a lot of times the poor people themselves join the capitalists in opposing liberation."

TOMÁS: "A lot of times, just for a few pennies offered by the powerful, the poor support the powerful."

PANCHO: "Anyone who defends the Gospels has everyone against him, rich and poor."

ÓSCAR: "And you can notice this right here on these Solentiname Islands, even though there are so few of us. Even us poor people criticize people who are trying to do us good. We criticize people who are fighting to free us from the exploitation that we all suffer."

Another one added: "The same thing happens with the spies, who are often poor people, and out of innocence, out of dumbness, they're helping the exploitation. They're going against their own interests, against their own brothers and sisters."

When they persecute you in one town,
flee to another;
for in truth I tell you
that the Son of Man is going to come
before you have travelled
through all the towns of Israel.

I said that this was a very mysterious passage, that I myself was not very clear about it, and that we ought to meditate in order to try to discover its meaning.

There was a long silence. Afterwards ELVIS spoke: "It seems that when he comes all the towns won't be liberated yet. Isn't that what he's saying?"

OLIVIA: "It seems to me that anyone who is preaching the Gospel has a right to protect his life, and if they're persecuting him in one town he ought to go to another town, instead of dying there without liberating anything. If you don't succeed in one place, go to another. He says that they won't cover all the places before he comes, because liberation is very slow, because it's so hard to struggle with the masses, and then you move ahead so little. And if the best leaders are often killed, as always happens, then you have to retreat. And his coming is bound to happen anyway ... "

TOMÁS: "And we won't have finished travelling to all the places. We'll be left who knows where ... "

Someone: "That's all very good, it's all very clear ... "

ALEJANDRO: "It may be clear, but it's not good."

Another one said: "It means that the struggle will be a long one and that all the towns won't be liberated before he comes. But when he does come everything will be solved."

No disciple is greater than his teacher,
and no servant is greater than his master.
The disciple must try to
  become like his teacher,
and the servant like his master.
If the lord of the house is called Beelzebub,
what will they call the members
  of his family?

I said that Beelzebub, one of the names that they gave to the devil, meant "lord of the house," and that Jesus, when he says that he, the lord of the house, is called Beelzebub, is making a pun. This is a sample of Jesus' humor. Even though he's talking of persecutions, he makes a joke. The Jews made a play on words between this word and another that sounds a lot like it which meant: "Lord of shit."

Another one: "Sometimes the disciple is greater than the teacher, when instead of calling him Beelzebub they call him Your Excellency ... "

And another: "If the disciple can't be greater than the teacher, we also should expect all kinds of attacks without being demoralized."

TOMÁS: "We have to bear up."

28.

Which One to Fear

(MATTHEW 10:26–31)

Therefore do not fear the people.
For there is no secret
that will not be discovered,
and nothing hidden
that will not be revealed.
What I tell you in darkness,
say it by the light of day;
and what I tell you in secret
shout it from the housetops.
Do not fear those who kill the body
but cannot kill the soul;
rather fear the one
that can destroy the body
* and the soul in hell.*

TOMÁS PEÑA spoke first: "The one you have to fear is the Evil One, because the Evil One is a spirit like God. He was with God and he learned a lot from him. And since he is evil he can do all kinds of evil to us."

His son FELIPE: "The Evil One is the spirit that

controls people, and this evil spirit works through the people who obey him. We ought to be afraid of anyone who works with the evil spirit, which isn't the spirit of love."

ÓSCAR: "I also think Jesus is referring here to hypocrisy, because there are times when you do things in secret, when you say: 'I'm doing this on the sly and screwing the others.' But it says here that there's nothing hidden that won't be found out."

LAUREANO: "I believe one thing: Here it tells who we should be afraid of. . . . I think it's that we shouldn't be afraid of anyone, that we should fight against injustice whenever we can. The way it says here: What I say to you in secret you shout it. More than anything else, it's this, I think: Denounce injustice."

ALEJANDRO: "One sentence here is very clear: 'Therefore do not fear the people.' The fear you have that they're going to do you some harm. And when are they going to do you harm? When you're against certain systems, certain injustices. That is, we're absolutely forbidden to be afraid of telling the truth, of being against anything that will endanger us, even our lives. It's clear that for the sake of justice we have to risk even our bodies. They can kill the body but they can't kill the cause for which we fight. And it spreads even wider: The Gospel tells us some words here in secret that we're supposed to shout."

Another boy said: "I think like you, Alejandro,

that here, the government we have in Nicaragua, it does whatever it wants with us, with the people, and because we're afraid we don't fight against these injustices. According to what it says here we shouldn't be afraid of that, because if they're doing an injustice to the people we should fight. And all right, let's die, the body isn't worth anything and they can destroy our bodies but not our souls. It seems to me then that we ought to fight and not submit."

ARMANDO: "Another important thing that I see it says here: Some may lose their bodies and others may lose their bodies and their souls together. If you support exploitation you lose both, body and soul."

I said it was also interesting to see that Jesus doesn't contrast the soul and the body, in the sense that it doesn't matter to lose your body if you save your immortal soul. For Jesus the saving or the losing is for the body and the soul together, that is, the whole person. And Jesus didn't really use the word 'soul' in the sense in which we use it, because the word didn't exist among the Jews. Instead he used the word 'life.' What he is telling us is that there is a death that does not destroy a person and that we shouldn't fear it. But there is another death that does destroy the whole person.

ALEJANDRO: "As I see it, the Gospel tells us not to be afraid of people. And when it tells us something it's so that we can practice it and speak about it. Now, I'm not clear about that business of the secret. Can the secret be the Gospel . . . ?"

OLIVIA: "I think so, because the words of the Gospels are a mysterious thing, a secret. And this is something that everyone doesn't know. There are only a few that receive this secret. And it's at the bottom of our hearts that we get to hear this secret word of Jesus. But what Jesus told us in private, we have to make public, and it will have an influence even on politics and it will change society."

JULIO MAIRENA said: "This is like when Ernesto announced that he was a socialist. It was a secret that wasn't supposed to be kept a secret but to be spread around."

I said that Jesus had to tell his message to a few people and because of the historical conditions of that time, his message could not influence politics. Up till now the Gospels have been followed only individually or in small communities (monasteries and convents), but we see that the time is now coming when it should be made *public*—in political life and in social life. Now the historical conditions allow the change of attitude to be a change in society as a whole.

ARMANDO: "And injustice and exploitation can't be kept hidden all the time. The poor have been deceived. They were made to believe they were poor because of bad luck or because of God's will. Now all the oppressed are beginning to realize that they're being exploited, and maybe that's also why he says that there's nothing hidden that won't get known. And the Revolution must be shouted from the housetops."

ANTENOR: "He didn't use any propaganda or any kind of broadcasting or even write a book. That's why he says he whispered it. But it was so that we could broadcast it without being afraid."

You can buy two little birds
for a penny, can't you?
But not one of them falls to earth
without your Father allowing it.

LAUREANO: "I think that here also he's telling us not to be afraid of anything, because just as God takes care of the little birds, they don't fall unless he allows it, so he'll take care of us so that we won't fall. We'll fall when we have to fall or when our fall does some good, and that isn't really a fall."

MANUEL: "We see clearly the importance that these people have in God's eyes when even the hairs on their head are counted one by one. And we must be conscious of how valuable we are."

Another one added: "It means each one of us is of tremendous importance to God."

And OLIVIA: "As I understand it, the Gospel tells us this so we know that we're worth so much, as Manuelito says. Because a person is the loveliest and most beloved creature of God.

He takes care of us, and we're so valuable that even when we die we're not dead. We're just living more, and that's why we shouldn't be afraid."

I said we shouldn't be afraid not because nothing bad is going to happen to us but because nothing can happen to us that isn't the will of God. But this is the same as saying that nothing really bad can happen to us, because God is in control of the whole universe, even the flight of a little bird he has to watch over, and God is love.

ARMANDO: "Even the little birds that are worth hardly anything in the market are worth a lot to God. How much more must people be worth to him, although for the exploiters people aren't worth anything. They buy them very cheap."

One of the girls: "And that's a lovely comparison with the little birds."

29.

Jesus a Cause of Division

(MATTHEW 10:34–37)

Before reading the passage we were going to comment on, ÓSCAR had seen the title and exclaimed: "I don't understand this! He came to bring unity. Why does it say here that he's a cause of division. He's supposed to be love!"

I said that first we ought to read it. We read this brief passage from Matthew, four verses, and went on to comment on them:

> *Do not believe that*
> *I have come to bring peace to earth;*
> *for I have come to bring*
> *not peace but the sword.*

ANTENOR said: "Injustice had always reigned on earth. He is coming to put an end to that state of affairs. So he's coming to fight. But he's not going to be fighting all alone. He does it with us."

MARCELINO: "He brought a very sharp weapon, which is his word. He brought that weapon for us. And it's what we're receiving here."

One said: "Jesus is against being a conformist. That is why he said he didn't come to bring peace."

Another said: "There are people who want to live in peace, to have no problems ... "

And young ARMANDO: "There are two kinds of peace. There's a peace that's simply to accept injustice, to remain quiet while the exploitation goes on. And there's another peace, the one we get after we achieve justice, when things get straightened out."

LAUREANO: "It seems to me that Jesus is teaching here that just because he was Jesus he wasn't going to change things, bang!, to divide everything up. On the contrary, it's up to us to fight so that we can have peace."

ARMANDO: "Because you have to fight to reach that peace, right?"

LAUREANO went on: "Yes, you have to fight hard in every country to get justice established throughout the world."

ALEJANDRO said: "Another thing that I see is that you can't have peace if you really love your neighbor. Even when there's peace in a community, like here in Solentiname, where life is peaceful and happy because we're all at peace, even here, deep down you have the great worry, the uneasiness ... because you see injustice more clearly. And the cause of this worry, I think, is love. And you can say, then, that this person is not completely at peace because he is concerned about others. And it would be too bad if we were all calm."

Another said: "Since Jesus has come to bring a change, that is, a Revolution, he wasn't coming to bring peace but war."

I: "It's clear that as long as there is a class of oppressors and a class of the oppressed, you can't want to have peace between oppressors and oppressed, because that means to want to have oppression. But if we want the oppressed class to be freed so that there won't any longer be oppressors and oppressed, then we really do not want peace."

And ÓSCAR said: "Ah, now I understand. What Jesus brought was unity for some but not for all. For some—those who are on the side of love. He's the cause of division because he's the cause of unity."

I have come to set the
man against his father,
the daughter against her mother,
the daughter-in-law against
her mother-in-law:
so that each one will have for enemies
the members of his own family.

LAUREANO: "This seems to be against love, but as a matter of fact you shouldn't always be stuck to your family, to your own kind. You should be for everyone, for your blood brothers as well as for those who aren't your blood brothers, because these are your brothers, too."

Another of the boys said: "It happens sometimes that the father is an exploiter and the son is a good Christian and the son has to be against him."

ANTENOR: "This division within families has to happen. And whenever there are new ideas that go against tradition, the parents are almost always in favor of the traditional ways and the new ideas are against them."

LAUREANO: "As I see it here he's setting the young against the old: the son against the father, the daughter against the mother, the daughter-in-law against the mother-in-law. It seems that Jesus sees that the division he's going to cause in families will be mainly a division between generations. And it's because the young people are the ones who are almost always with the Revolution, and not the old people."

I said that that division in families of which Jesus spoke was seen clearly in Cuba at the time of the Revolution. Many families were divided, and whenever there is a Revolution this has to happen.

LEONEL: "How long? Until we've reached unity, right? Because it can't always be like that. Division happens so that later there will be unity, a final peace."

ARMANDO: "But meanwhile Jesus comes to

break the unity of the family, which was considered a very sacred thing, and since the family is the basis of society he comes to upset all of society. Here he publicly declares himself a disturber of social peace."

ANTENOR: "That business about the family I see also as a way of talking about the class struggle."

He who loves his father or his mother
 more than me
is not worthy of me;
and he who loves his son or his daughter
 more than me
is not worthy of me.

One of the young men said: "There are a lot of people here who are too attached to their families."

And OLIVIA, who hadn't spoken up to then, said: "Jesus isn't saying here that we have to love the God of heaven and forget about people, but that's how it has been understood in our traditional religion. And so for example a man leaves his money to 'God,' as he says, because he'd rather leave it to God than to the poor. No, I think that when Jesus is talking about love for him, he's putting himself in the place of the poor, and of our neighbor in general. And what he means is that we should love all people, all our neighbors, and not just those in our family."

Another added: "To love God is to love your brother, isn't it?"

And LAUREANO: "Your brother, but not your brother because he's the son of your mother, but because he's your brother who is everybody."

FELIPE: "Some think they're pleasing God with prayers or songs, but singing to God is loving your brother."

And one of the girls: "It's a matter of loving not only our family and your friends but of loving everybody, and that's hard."

ARMANDO: "And speaking of the God of heaven—the God of heaven doesn't exist, or at least the only way we can know him is as he is made flesh in other people."

FELIPE: "Anyone who loves other people, practically speaking, already knows God."

I said that was exactly what Saint John said.

And ALEJANDRO: "It's because God is love. Anyone who loves knows him because he has known love."

JULIO: "The sword splits, divides, and now I see why he says that he brought the sword."

GLORIA: "The sword of love."

EPILOGUE

In October 1977, during a period of countrywide up-heaval, the Nicaraguan National Guard ravaged the Solentiname community. In December, writing from Costa Rica, Cardenal explained in a "Letter to the People of Nicaragua" why he had joined the Sandinista guerrillas. The following translation by William Barbieri is reprinted with permission of the National Catholic Reporter, Box 281, Kansas City, MO 64141.

Twelve years ago I arrived at Solentiname with two companions to found a small, contemplative community. Contemplation means union with God. We soon became aware that this union with God brought us before all else into union with the peasants, very poor and very abandoned, who lived dispersed along the shores of the archipelago.

Contemplation also brought us to the revolution. It had to be that way. If not, it would have been fake contemplation. My old novice master, Thomas Merton, the inspirer and spiritual director of our foundation, told me that in Latin America I could not separate myself from political strife.

In the beginning we would have preferred a revolution with nonviolent methods. But we soon began to

267

realize that at this time in Nicaragua a nonviolent struggle is not feasible. Even Gandhi would agree with us. The truth is that all authentic revolutionaries prefer nonviolence to violence; but they are not always free to choose.

The Gospel was what most radicalized us politically. Every Sunday in Mass we discussed the Gospel in a dialogue with the peasants. With admirable simplicity and profound theology, they began to understand the core of the Gospel message: the announcement of the kingdom of God, that is, the establishment on this earth of a just society, without exploiters or exploited, with all goods in common, just like the society in which the first Christians lived. But above all else the Gospel taught us that the word of God is not only to be heard, but also to be put into practice.

As the peasants of Solentiname got deeper and deeper into the Gospel, they could not help but feel united to their brother and sister peasants who were suffering persecution and terror, who were imprisoned, tortured, murdered; they were violated and their homes were burnt. They also felt solidarity with all who with compassion for their neighbor were offering their lives. For this solidarity to be real, they had to lay security, and life, on the line.

In Solentiname it was well known that we were not going to enjoy peace and tranquillity if we wanted to put into practice the word of God. We knew that the hour of sacrifice was going to arrive. This hour has now come. Now in our community everything is over.

There a school of primitive painting became famous throughout the world. Paintings, woodwork, and various handicrafts from Solentiname are sold not only in Managua, but also in New York, Washington, Paris, Venezuela, Puerto Rico, Switzerland, and Germany. Lately peasants from Solentiname had begun to write beautiful poetry. Their poems were published in Nicaragua and other countries.

Several films were made in Solentiname, one of them by BBC in London. Much has been written about Solentiname in various languages; records have been made, even in German. We have in that distant corner of the lake a great library gathered during a lifetime. We had a collection of pre-Columbian art found in Solentiname that grew through the years. We had a large guest house with plenty of beds for visitors. We had ovens for ceramics and a large shop for all kinds of handicrafts. There we worked with wood, leather, copper, bronze, and silver. We were also developing communal work for young peasants through a cooperative. The cooperative, with the help of a German institution, was about ready to begin a dairy and factory of European-style cheese.

It was said in Germany: "Solentiname is everywhere, it is the beginning of a more human world. It is a Christian life—not just waiting for a better world, but working for their neighbor's peace, for peace in nature, for peace within the community." In Venezuela it was said that "Solentiname is something so God-like and so much of this world that it is a place where po-etry, painting, and the harvest do not divide people into poets and farmers, but constitute the solidarity of one life." Now all that is over.

Twelve years ago, when the apostolic nuncio approved my project to found a new monastery, he told me that he would have preferred that the community be established in a less remote place than Solentiname, because there we would have no visitors. The truth is that we were always flooded with visitors from Nicaragua and other countries. Many times they were people who arrived in Nicaragua only to visit Solentiname; sometimes they arrived directly by way of Los Chiles or San Carlos, without any interest in even visiting Managua. Abundant correspondence from all parts of the world arrived in Solentiname.

But now brush will grow once again where our community used to be, just as it did before our arrival. There, there was a peasant mass, there were paintings, statues, books, records, classes, smiles of beautiful children, poetry, song. Now all that is left is the savage beauty of nature. I lived a very happy life in that near paradise that was Solentiname. But I was always ready to sacrifice it all. And now we have.

One day it happened that a group of boys and girls from Solentiname, because of profound convictions and after having let it mature for a long time, decided to take up arms. Why did they do it? They did it for only one reason: for their love for the kingdom of God, for the ardent desire that a just society be implanted, a real and concrete kingdom of God here on earth. When the time came, these boys and girls fought with great valor, but they also fought as Christians. That morning at San Carlos, they tried several times with a loudspeaker to reason with the guards so they might not have to fire a single shot. But the guards responded to their reasoning with submachine gunfire. With great regret, they also were forced to shoot.

Alejandro Guevara, one of those from my community, entered the building when in it there were no longer any but dead or wounded soldiers. He was going to set fire to it so that there would be no doubt about the success of the assault, but out of consideration for the wounded, he did not do it. Because the building was not burned, it was officially denied that it was taken. I congratulate myself that these young Christians fought without hate—above all, without hate for the wounded guards, poor peasants like themselves, also exploited. It is horrible that there are dead and wounded. We wish that there were not a struggle in Nicaragua, but this does not depend upon the oppressed people that are only defending themselves.

Some day there will be no more war in Nicaragua, no more peasant guards killing other peasants. Instead there will be an abundance of schools, hospitals, and clinics for everyone, food adequate for everyone, art and entertainment. But most important, there will be love among all.

Now the repression that has gone on so long in the North has arrived at Solentiname. A tremendous number of peasants have had to flee, others are in exile, remembering those beautiful islands with their now destroyed homes. They would be there yet, living tranquil lives, dedicated to their daily tasks. But they thought of their neighbor, and of Nicaragua, and began to work for them.

I do not think about the reconstruction of our small community of Solentiname. I think of a task much more important that we all have—the reconstruction of the whole country.

On July 19, 1979, the Sandinista revolution was victorious. Many of the Solentiname community participated in the struggle against the Somoza dictatorship. Ernesto Cardenal is now Minister of Culture of Nicaragua.

Also from Orbis . . .

Tissa Balasuriya
THE EUCHARIST AND HUMAN LIBERATION
"Balasuriya, one of Asia's most productive Christian theologians, is now at the Centre for Society and Religion in Colombo, Sri Lanka. In this disarmingly straightforward and profoundly disturbing book he makes a bold contribution to the contemporary debate about what roles Christians and the Church should play in the struggles for universal justice, equitable distribution of the world's goods, and the liberation of oppressed nations and social classes. Balasuriya shows how the chief liturgical service of the Church, the celebration of the Eucharist (Holy Communion) could become a major revolutionary force, challenging and empowering millions of people to contribute to the birth of a new world order. He argues simply and forcefully for a transformation of Christianity much more radical than has yet been brought about by modern church councils and commissions. This book should find a wide audience among non-Christians and Christians alike; it is appropriate for the general public and for both graduate and undergraduate teachers and students of religion, economics, contemporary history and cultures, and the political and social sciences."

Choice
184pp. Paper $6.95

John Eagleson and
Sergio Torres, eds.
THE CHALLENGE OF BASIC
CHRISTIAN COMMUNITIES
The major papers from the meeting of the
Ecumenical Association of Third World
Theologians held in São Paulo, Brazil, 1979.
This is another of Orbis's documentation of
Third World theology.

The contents include: *The Latin American
Woman* by Cora Ferro, *Current Events in Latin
America* by Enrique Dussel, *Latin American
Protestantism* by Carmelo E. Alvarez, *The Irruption of the Poor in Latin America and the Christian Communities of the Common People* by
Gustavo Gutiérrez, *Theological Characteristics
of a Grassroots Church* by Leonardo Boff,
O.F.M., *Fundamental Questions in Ecclesiology* by José Míguez Bonino, *The Witness
of the Church in Latin America* by Jon Sobrino,
S.J., *The Church Born of the People in
Nicaragua* by Miguel d'Escoto, M.M., *Give Us
This Day Our Daily Bread* by Samuel Rayan,
*From Geneva to Sao Paulo: A Dialogue Between Black Theology and Latin American
Liberation Theology* by James H. Cone, *Final
Document.*

352pp. $9.95

Plácido Erdozaín
ARCHBISHOP ROMERO: Martyr of Salvador
"The author of this book, Father Erdozaín, is an Augustinian priest who worked with Archbishop Romero. He has written not so much a biography of him—though a revealing and sympathetic personal portrait does emerge —as an account of his struggle with oppressors of that unhappy nation. It is, in effect, a history of the country since 1932, and it is packed densely with information, facts, figures, and names —including those of the 'fourteen families' who control its destiny and stifle any slightest move toward freedom. It is perhaps the most compact and convenient source from which to learn the story of El Salvador and its agony."   *The Catholic Review*

"An excellent source of information on the events and people in El Salvador and, in view of the political importance of that country at the moment, it is my feeling that it belongs in libraries of this country, for there just isn't much else available which will provide the inquiring reader with information on the situation."
Best Sellers
128pp. Paper $4.95